HEREFORD CHORAL SOCIETY

An Unfinished History

TIMOTHY DAY

HEREFORD CHORAL SOCIETY

Published by the committee of Hereford Choral Society

ISBN 978 0 9927781 0 1

Designed and typeset by Timothy Symons

Printed in Britain by Butler, Tanner and Dennis
Caxton Road, Frome, Somerset BA11 1NF

Timothy Day was an organ scholar at St John's College, Oxford where he read Music and then studied composition. He has worked as a waiter and in a chocolate factory but spent most of his life as a music curator in the British Library. He is a cultural historian and the author of *A Century of Recorded Music: Listening to Musical History* (Yale University Press, 2000).

Between 2006 and 2011 he was a visiting senior research fellow at King's College London. In 2006–7 he held a Leverhulme Research Fellowship to begin collecting material for a study he is now completing on the performing styles of English cathedral choirs in the twentieth century.

Contents

For all past and present members of
Hereford Choral Society
(and their musical advisers)

Preface

How old is the Hereford Choral Society?

In the 1870s the members of Hereford Choral Society began to be rather proud of its longevity. On the leaflet for the performance of *Judas Maccabaeus* in 1878 they proclaimed 'established 1838'. In the years following they repeated this; in 1882 they talked of their 'Forty-Fourth Season'.[1] And there it is on the printed Rule Book 'as revised on 2 February 1900', 'established 1838'.[2]

Sometimes confusion arose. In 1888 they announced that they were celebrating their forty-*ninth* season. This may have been through the mixing up of calendar years and academic years. The forty-fourth season was 1882; the forty-fifth season was 1883–4. At any rate the concert notices of the 1890s always claimed that the Society had been founded in 1839.[3]

In the leaflets of the 1900s the committee member responsible for advertising can't make up his mind; for several years running 1838 oscillates with 1839: spring is 1838, autumn is 1839. The bills for 1917 and 1919 are extant and both give 1838.[4] And at the annual general meeting in October 1919 Percy Hull spoke of the privilege it was to conduct a Society which had existed for eighty-one years – that is, since 1838 – and which had such a fine reputation. He repeated this at the annual meeting in 1922 and hoped that the Society would still be flourishing at its centenary in 1938 and far beyond.[5]

But then the Society's printed accounts for 1 October 1922 to 31 December 1923 assert 'established 1837'.[6] Why was this? There seems to be no document extant which gives any reasons for the change. But a letter produced by the Roneo method of duplication was sent out by the Secretary in 1922 – it has the handwritten annotation 'May?' – to give news and details of the autumn concert to existing subscribers. The letterhead, 'Hereford Choral Society/Est 1838', had come out very faintly, the date only just visible. So someone – the painstaking secretary perhaps – carefully wrote over the year on each copy of the letter, choosing a nice blue ink to match the Roneo colour.[7] The diligent scribe, though, made a mistake and put *1837* instead of 1838. The next concert programme extant is that for November 1923 (*The Golden Legend*) and that says 'established 1837'.[8] And 'established 1837' it remained. The 'centenary' was celebrated in 1937, the 150th birthday in 1987 and the 175th birthday in 2012.

But, as the historical documents make clear, the Choral Society did actually begin in 1838. The first public performances in which members of the Choral Society took part seem to have been in June 1838.[9] Among the Society's papers is a volume of eighteenth-century scores acquired in 1869 of Handel's Four Coronation Anthems. On the cover is a printed book-plate: 'HEREFORD CHORAL SOCIETY, ESTABLISHED MARCH MDCCCXXXVIII.'[10] The actual 175th anniversary of the founding of the Society is 2013.

It all goes to show how important it is for Hon. Secretaries to remember their reading glasses.

The conductors of Hereford Choral Society

1838–42	John Hunt (1806–42)
1843–77	George Townshend Smith (1813–77)
1877–89	Langdon Colborne (1835–89)
1889–1917	George Robertson Sinclair (1863–1917)
1918–49	Percy Hull (1878–1968)
1950–56	Meredith Davies (1922–2005)
1956–66	Melville Cook (1912–93)
1966–74	Richard Lloyd (*b* 1933)
1974–2001	Roy Massey (*b* 1934)
2001–	Geraint Bowen (*b* 1963)

Acknowledgements

I am very grateful to Clare Wichbold, the chair of the committee of Hereford Choral Society, for inviting me to write this history to mark its 175th anniversary. I'm especially grateful to Marian Hale for supplying me with the Society's working files and for making many suggestions, and to Helen Powers and Clare Stevens for overseeing the production of the book. I should like to thank Mark Ewins for arranging the distribution of a questionnaire to members of the Choral Society. I didn't use the results of the questionnaire directly but the views expressed in it informed my discussion of various points and I should like to thank everyone who took the trouble to respond.

The Society's own papers are deposited in Hereford Cathedral Library and I'm most grateful to the Librarian, Rosemary Firman, and to the Archivist, Rosalind Caird, for their expert assistance as well as their constant encouragement.

I owe many thanks to Dr Derek Foxton, who was most generous in showing me his archive of photographs and providing images for the book; to Gordon Taylor, who photographed all the images from the cathedral's archives (both of them also took new additional photographs); and to Timothy Symons, who designed the book.

I also offer my thanks to the staff of Herefordshire Record Office and of Hereford Library, and also to Brian Crosby, John Eisel, Liz Pitman, Guy Rawlinson, Jo Swindells, Alan Thurlow, Michael Trott, Clare Wichbold and Barbara Young.

Timothy Day

The Nineteenth-Century Choral Society

Singing in Hereford in the 1830s and 40s

That middle-class families in Hereford in the 1830s expected their daughters to receive instruction in music is quite clear from the notices in the *Hereford Journal*. There was Spring Field House, for example, at Charlton Kings in Cheltenham – 'delightfully situated and admirably adapted to the health and comfort of the Pupils, without the great expense so generally attendant on a Liberal Education' – which emphasised 'the acquirement of the modern Languages and Music, as also a sound knowledge of the Scriptures'. And Mrs Hart would announce that at *her* academy, Arcadia House, instruction was provided 'in all the branches of English Literature' and in 'French, Music, Dancing, and Drawing'. At Upper Cottage in Newent, devoted to the 'ornamental and useful instruction of young Ladies', attention was drawn to the special provision provided in the teaching of 'Thorough Bass'.[1] And if a governess were seeking a situation in Hereford she would be keen to demonstrate that she recognised the priorities expected by potential employers: 'the young Lady is competent to instruct in Music, the rudiments of French and Drawing, with the general routine of useful Education'.[2]

All these strenuous efforts towards musical accomplishment though were made not for exhibitionism in the public arena but for modest cultivation in the domestic sphere. Chiefly of course to entrance the young gentlemen. Or at least one young gentleman. Young ladies might open their mouths wide in the Festival Chorus it was true, but those ladies – those 'Celebrated Females' – were from Birmingham and from Lancashire.[3] In Hereford they did things differently.

Their mothers – the older ladies – *had* sung. Of course they had. They had discernment and exquisite taste and judgement in all matters musical. But they felt it their duty now to encourage their daughters, not to try and put them in the shade. They could go with them to Mrs Bayliss's music shop. ('Mrs Bayliss? Yes you do, dear. Miss M'Cann, Maria M'Cann, as she was before her nuptials last Christmas. No dear, on the *Worcester* Road.') Mrs Bayliss regu-larly received popular and fashionable music from Town. Any lady honouring her with a call, Mrs Bayliss advertised, would have the advantage of hearing any piece or song she wished to purchase first played over on the harp or pianoforte. But there were still pitfalls to which mothers could alert musical daughters. 'Now there, in that song, Dorothea, is the *tessitura* quite right for your mezzo?'[4]

Gentlemen did not sing. They didn't play either. Very few of them. English attitudes towards musical education for boys throughout the eighteenth century, which only began to be questioned in the later nineteenth century and to be shed only in the twentieth, were stated clearly in an influential book on education published in 1693. Boys and young men in England should indeed develop some prac-tical skills unrelated to their study of Latin, Greek and mathematics such as painting, gardening, joinery or even gem-polishing. But they are not required to study music: 'It wastes so much of a young man's time to gain but a moderate skill in it, and engages often in such odd company that many think it much better spared.'[5] That professional musicians were artisans – *should* be artisans – was cer-tainly generally accepted in Hereford in the 1830s. For a well-to-do gentleman to take up a musical instrument was a kind of revolt against the natural order of things. There's a glimpse of this in an advertisement in the *Hereford Journal* in December 1835: 'TRUM-PETER wants a Place as trumpeter, in a Nobleman's or Gentleman's family in the County of Hereford, a middle-aged, well-educated single Man. He has lived many years in his last place, (in the vicin-ity of Ludlow) which he has quitted solely on account of his Master's having determined henceforth to *be his own Trumpeter*.'[6] The poor trumpeter's puzzlement and exasperation can be felt in his italics.

There were certainly Englishman of the first half of the nine-teenth century who would have agreed with Mr Collins in *Pride and Prejudice* that music was 'a very innocent diversion, and perfectly compatible with the profession of a clergyman.'[7] Musical accom-plishment was more or less acceptable in a clergyman, provided the interest was not excessive. It must be restrained, rather like demon-strations of piety by young gentlemen. Even so very few clergymen really did have any serious interest in music and fewer still any kind of practical ability. The reluctance of senior clergymen to encourage ordinands to acquire knowledge of music and some expertise as singers or players riled Sir Frederick Ouseley, the precentor at the cathedral from 1855 until his death in 1889: young men could not be expected 'to become musicians unless professional musicians aid them, teach them, encourage them, and co-operate with them'.[8] The trouble was that senior figures in the Church of England – very few senior figures in any English profession – ever had any contact with musicians. As they didn't with pastry-cooks.

Then there were the singers in the cathedral choir. The fortunes of the Choral Society have been so closely entwined with those of the cathedral choir that the singers in the stalls must be examined closely and their attitudes understood, and attitudes towards them too, if the fortunes of the chorus are to be grasped. In 1851 Ouseley called the boys in English cathedral choirs 'too often mere rabble' and it's not possible to be sure that he would not have applied this description to the boys of Hereford at this time. In 1851 Ouseley was in Germany, and in Dresden and Leipzig he found boys whose intonation was 'so true and the style so tasteful and refined, and the quality so rich and full and round, that it leaves nothing to be desired.' He suspected that they were chosen from 'a somewhat higher class of Society' than choristers in England were and that this was the underlying reason for 'their more refined style'.[9] The boys in English cathedrals in Ouseley's days were nearly always from poor families. In most cathedrals they would be given what was called a 'commercial' education preparing them for some trade or other when they left the choir at fourteen or fifteen. Hereford though did have an excellent school and a small number of boys would be prepared for Oxford or Cambridge.

A visitor from Boston, Massachusetts came to Europe in 1852 with the express purpose of listening to choral singing, of hearing choirs of all kinds. He went to Evensong at Worcester Cathedral in January 1852. Everything was characterised by 'rapidity of utterance'; the psalms were carelessly enunciated and the speed at which the words were gabbled prevented any attempt at expressiveness of any kind. The services at York Minster, he was told, were the best sung of any in England; well, the rapid chanting was certainly no worse than the similar gabbling he'd heard at other English cathedrals, but the 'terrible roughness' of the boys' voices was enough 'to tear out one's soul'. Just before he left London to return home he ran into the Austrian composer Sigismund Neukomm and asked him about English trebles. 'Boys' voices', that gentleman replied, 'are like cats' voices.' It was the shrillness and the screeching of English boys, Neukomm told him, that so got on Mendelssohn's nerves on one occasion in Exeter Hall in 1837 as he sat listening to a rehearsal of

St Paul. And Mendelssohn had wondered why on earth the English didn't follow the Germans and employ women for both soprano and alto parts.[10] S S Wesley, the organist at Hereford from 1832 until 1835, who was to become the most distinguished cathedral musician of the day in England, ascribed no particular value to boys' voices at all; he simply regretted that he had to use what he considered a 'poor substitute for the vastly superior quality and power of those of women'.[11]

When Mr Gardiner, a music-lover from Leicester, came into Hereford Cathedral in 1802 and asked a verger about the choir he was told that all the twelve singing men were 'gentlemen choristers', all graduates of the university. The visitor was very surprised. He'd never found any 'educated persons' appointed to such offices before. He eagerly went along one Sunday only to find an 'inferior performer' on the organ and no singing men in the choir at all. No, it was explained to him, on Sundays they have to be attending to their parish duties. But they did sing services with the boys on the other days.[12]

And so it was in the 1830s. Why was this? Why were the singing men at nearly all other cathedrals lay clerks, whereas the singing men at Hereford were clergymen, university graduates? This was simply because of a charter of 1395 granted by Richard II which had never been abolished. Several of the vicars had been choristers at Hereford and then, their musical and academic gifts being apparent, had been carefully taught – some of them had had extra coaching in the College of Vicars Choral – and proceeded to Oxford. And they had returned and spent their lives as vicars choral. Unlike their medieval predecessors they had to care after local parishes as well as sing. Their musical duties were not so heavy and so they had been given additional duties. Their salaries, which derived partly from ancient endowments, might have been adequate for single men living in the College but were insufficient for married men with families, constantly traipsing along muddy roads from their outlying parishes to the cathedral. Their music-making was inefficient, partly because the other work led to frequent absences from the choir-stalls, partly because their musical training had been inadequate. No doubt there were some good voices among them. But even those with good voices had not been given the appropriate tuition, neither musical nor vocal. They certainly loved music, and were much more musical and knowledgeable and educated than most lay clerks of the time, though not such musical experts as they thought they were. Not only was their music-making not as good as it should have been, but the vicars choral were brittle characters. In an age when musicians were held in such low regard by English men and women they were acutely aware of their low status within the

1844
Hereford Choral Society
Michaelmas Special Meeting. October 1st
Selection from Samson
Overture   Handel
Chorus – "O first created beam"
Chorus – "Let their celestial concerts"   "
Chorus – "Then round about the starry throne"   "
         "Fixed in his everlasting seat"
Anthem – "Plead thou my cause"   Mozart
Solo – "In native worth" (Creation)   Haydn
Chorus – "The heavens are telling"   "
Hymn – "O come all ye faithful" Arranged by Novello
Coronation Anthem "Zadock the priest"   Handel
Chorus – "Hallelujah" (Mount of Olives)   Beethoven
Chorus – "Come gentle spring" (Seasons)   Haydn
Chorus – "Madlou"
Chorus – "We praise thee" (Dettingen Te Deum)   Handel
Chorus – "All the earth"   "
Chorus – "To thee all angels"   "
         "Day by Day"
         "O Lord in thee"   "
Anthem – "Glory be to God"   Haydn
National Anthem "God save the Queen" arranged by Novello

Details for the concert on 1 October 1844 in the
minute-book of the Hereford Philharmonic Society

cathedral. They were hardly ever given promotion by the Chapter, hardly ever offered larger and more valuable benefices. As a future residentiary at Hereford conceded in 1843, the Vicars Choral 'are looked upon as the drudges of the Chapter, as an order of men inferior in caste'.[13] The social status of musicians generally inevitably coloured the Chapter's attitudes to the vicars choral. When it was proposed that undergraduates at King's College, Cambridge should 'assist in' the choir in 1873 the Provost, Richard Okes, born in 1797, was exceedingly angry. He turned on the governing body: the young men were admitted into the College 'for distinct purposes and into a defined position in the Society'. The defined position of an undergraduate was not to consort with singing men whose other duties included working in the kitchens, tuning pianos, and polishing Fellows' shoes.[14] And yet, because of these anachronistic

statutes, the College of Vicars Choral controlled part of the funds required for the cathedral's music. The Precentor was the member of the Chapter who had responsibility for the services and the music. But he had, time out of mind, delegated this to the Succentor who was a member of the College of Vicars Choral. The organisational structure was entirely unfit for purpose.

And nobody knew what cathedrals were for. The industrial cities of the north, bursting at the seams, cried out for more resources. In attempting to address this problem the government wanted to make use of the riches of the Church, which lay with cathedrals. So ancient endowments were taken from the cathedrals just at a time when there was mounting concern about and interest in ceremonial, in music, in ancient liturgies, at a time when, at last, reform of the choral foundations, which had been called for for decades, seemed at last genuinely possible. Under the Cathedrals Act of 1840, it was generally thought, the College of Vicars Choral at Hereford had been abolished. But nobody was quite sure. The Dean thought it had been. The vicars choral thought not. Or at least they behaved as if a question about abolition were so absurd it would never occur to anyone in his right mind to ask it. In 1851 the Chapter swept the vicars choral aside and appointed a body of lay clerks. But nobody was training lay clerks and the pay was so low and the hours so inconvenient – with two choral services most days – that no ambitious young man would ever consider such work. And so, as in other cathedrals, the music remained poorly performed. The College of Vicars now did no more than intone the services. But they paid the singers. They still counted themselves the musical experts. They continued to point out failings, ignoring the fact that the music had been bad when they had total responsibility for it.

Because it all continued so unsatisfactorily, and the College went on repeating that 'it was never contemplated by the Cathedral Statutes to throw the principal part of the Choral Duty upon Laymen',[15] the Chapter in the end gave way to the College, the statues were redrafted in 1870 and the post of 'assistant vicar choral' was created, which post could be filled by either lay clerk or vicar choral.[16] For a time several excellent young ordained priests were appointed. But most left quickly, perhaps not enjoying the tension and evident dislike which existed between some of the members of the College and some in the Chapter. At any rate the supply quickly dried up. Gradually the authority of the College ebbed away and for most of the twentieth century all the singing men were lay clerks, and singers of increasing competence and skill. For a time though lay clerks and vicars choral sang together. But not very well together.

'Wouldn't it be a good idea for that vicar choral to move forward and stand beside the lay clerk he's singing with instead of remain-

Programme for 14 October 1845

ing in the higher stall in the row behind?' the Chapter asked the Custos of the College in 1873. The reply they received must have set the teeth on edge of even the most saintly member of the Chapter: 'It is with regret', the Custos answered, 'that I find myself unable to install Mr Duncombe in that portion of the Choir which you assign to him as it would have been a departure from ancient custom and involve a violation of the oath which I have taken as Custos to maintain the privileges of the College to the best of my power.' It was not the vicars' reading that in any of the modifications made to the original medieval statutes, the Custos explained, the Dean and Chapter had been empowered to 'degrade' the vicars 'below their proper rank' and place them 'on the same level as the Deacons and lay assistants'.[17]

Like Hereford at this time, Wells Cathedral had 'priest vicars' singing in the choir together with lay clerks. In 1883 one of them bitterly pointed out that the Chapter made no distinction whatever between himself, 'a Cambridge MA in Holy Orders', and the carpenters, shoemakers, stonemasons and other tradesmen with whom he sang.[18] Whatever the logic or accuracy of the vicars' comments on the singing of the lay clerks and the boys and their recurrent quibbling over the particular interpretation of clauses in ancient ordinances the attitude of at least some of them was inevitably coloured by an emotional undercurrent of smouldering quivering

resentment. Most educated gentlemen could not disguise the slight suspicion and disdain they felt towards performing musicians even when they did wear a clerical collar.

So a few clergymen sang in Hereford in the 1830s and middle-class girls sang at home. And a few families of all kinds at home would make music together. Didn't the brewers and leather-workers of Hereford sing? At any rate not like the men and women did in Manchester and other industrial centres. There on Sunday evenings you would hear the 'Hallelujah Chorus' and a few hymns roared out from the singing saloons attached to public houses. But not in Hereford. What about the folk-songs and the carols that were collected only decades later? What about those musicians at Weobley singing 'The Wife of Wisher's Well' and 'I'll bind my petticoat' and 'Cold blows the wind' and 'Joseph being an old man truly', all those tunes that Mrs Leather and Vaughan Williams heard seventy years later? Some of the villagers and the gypsies would sing all the time when they were working, when they were there in the hop-fields. They loved the music and they used the music. But they didn't stand on a stage and perform it.[19]

So who *was* going to sing in this Choral Society?

The formation of the Choral Society

It was a bleak month in Hereford, that February of 1838. At the beginning of the month it had been bitterly cold, with the Wye frozen from bank to bank from the medieval bridge to Belmont. In the parish of St Peter's they'd had to deliver soup to 250 of the poorest families. But then, all of a sudden, it turned unseasonably mild. At daybreak on that Thursday, the 8th it would have been, the ice on the river began to heave and at eight o'clock, at breakfast time, there was a mighty crash and the ice split into a thousand pieces and vast fragments of it crashed into each other and into the bridge too. In the afternoon the clouds parted and the river became an expanse of rough broken snowy ice, sparkling like crystals in the sun. Throughout the day people came out onto the bridge just to watch. 'Truly sublime', literary types exclaimed.[20] Truly muddy it certainly was. There was mud and water everywhere that weekend.

But on the Monday evening a number of intrepid members of the St Peter's Reading Association ventured out to hear a lecture on the obscure topic of 'antient music'. This was given by the new organist at the cathedral. John Hunt described the music in far-off times among the Jews, the Greeks and the Egyptians. Ancient Jewish music he considered of a very superior character and he described the music in Solomon's Temple and the Levites, arrayed in white linen, with cymbals and psalteries and harps, standing at the east end of

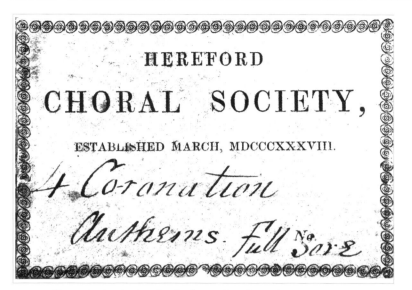

The 1860s book-plate for the Society's eighteenth-century scores

the altar, and with them a hundred and twenty trumpeters and with these instruments of music the singers joining in and praising the Lord: *for his mercy endureth for ever.* And Mr Hunt played specimens of ancient Greek and Hebrew music on the pianoforte, but, because there's so little of this music extant, he also played some Irish airs, which cheered everybody up no end.

His lecture was really about the power of music, how music was able to change people's lives. And he concluded by noting that it was not uncommon nowadays to find towns not larger than Hereford which had established their own choral society. This is what the city of Hereford needed, and he was going to use his best endeavours to follow their good example. What could be more calculated 'to raise the mind from earth to heaven … than the performances of the choruses of the great Masters'? And everyone clapped enthusiastically and before the evening was out several members of the Association had stepped forward and asked if they could join.[21]

What was this Reading Association? It was founded the year before at the prompting of the Vicar of St Peter's in order to afford 'the means of acquiring religious and scientific knowledge to the humbler classes of the city'. Thoroughgoing parliamentary educational reform was still a long way off – it was only with the Education Act of 1870 that national elementary education was established; it was only with the Act of 1891 that free elementary education was provided for everyone.

In an introductory lecture he gave in April 1837, the Dean of Hereford outlined what he took to be the main object of the Association, namely 'the promotion of general knowledge and useful learning on the one substantial and sure basis, the belief in a God, and submission to his revealed will'. It was hoped there might be lectures on chemistry and geology, for example, writing, mathematics, astronomy.[22] In the first term, every alternate Monday evening was going to be devoted to a course of lectures on botany. The Vicar of St Peter's was soon able to run a Greek course of which he became immensely proud.[23]

The aspirations of the St Peter's Library were similar to those of the Mechanics' Institutes which were being opened all over the place at that period. The first such institute had been opened in Edinburgh in 1821, but by the early 1840s there were 300 of them, concentrated in the North of England and particularly in Lancashire and the West Riding of Yorkshire. The idea had come from a Professor of Natural Philosophy in Glasgow called George Birkbeck, the Birkbeck who is commemorated in the name assumed in 1907 by the London Mechanics' Institute, Birkbeck College. In fact a few years later it was proposed that a Mechanics' Institute be established in Hereford. This was greeted initially with great suspicion at St Peter's and the Vicar became very defensive. His reading-room and library would remain far superior to a Mechanics' Institute, he was reported as saying; in his foundation knowledge is made 'the handmaid of Religion, without which science and learning are alike vain, useless, and unsatisfactory.' Eventually there was a public meeting. The Dean did not wish to discourage either the Vicar at St Peter's or those who were calling for the establishment of a Mechanics' Institute; in his view there was scope and an urgent need for both. As he saw it, the objects of Mechanics' Institutes were 'to teach the workman (be his trade what it may) those principles of science on which his works depends, to show him their practical application, and how he may make his knowledge of them profitable – to enable him thoroughly to understand his business, and to qualify him for making improvements in it, to teach him how he may advance himself in the world, and to give him an honourable and delightful employment for his leisure.'[24]

That was where a choral society fitted into the scheme, to provide 'honourable and delightful employment' for the leisure time of the younger men. The Hereford Choral Society did not constitute a class in the programme of either the Mechanics' Institute or the St Peter's Association. But it was a creature of the same impulses and concerns and aimed at the same section of society, young men 'of the humbler classes'.

In 1844 at Ross some of the young men of the Mechanics' Institute there came to Mr Moss, the organist of the parish church, and asked if they could form a choral society under his direction to meet regularly in the reading-room of the Institute. The *Hereford Times* reported that Mr Moss was only too pleased and cheerfully offered his services gratis in order that the young men should have a weekly opportunity of rational amusement, 'of spending an evening in the full enjoyment of those strains which have immortalised Handel's name, and which can only be surpassed by Cherubim and Seraphim in their everlasting song'. That was the promise the Ross Choral Society held out according to the *Hereford Times*.[25]

Rational amusement

And that was the phrase on everybody's lips, 'rational amusement' or 'rational recreation'. What did they mean by it? 'Rational' was a characteristic word of nineteenth-century discourse – rather like 'efficient' – and both had long become clichés before they were undermined by the dark forces of romanticism, by Freudian psychoanalysis, and by the terrible efficiency and irrationality of twentieth-century warfare.

The concept of 'rational amusement' arose from an awareness of the material advances that the industrial revolution was bringing to the world – at least to England – and a conviction that it was important that these should be accompanied by social improvements. Politicians, clergymen and commentators of all kinds looked round and saw poverty and squalor at the heart of economic success and what they perceived as physical and moral degeneracy. 'Rational amusement' outside the long hours of working people and tradesmen should be offered in an attempt to give men and women pleasure, education and moral constraints, and to assist social cohesion.

What kinds of activities constituted rational amusements? Sunday promenades in public gardens, like the French and the Germans, decently dressed, and the observation of the manners of social superiors, with the consumption by the *pater familias*, if any liquor at all were contemplated, of a glass of light beer. Games like cricket in the summer, 'this manly recreation' as the *Hereford Journal* called it in 1836.[26] Tea parties in the winter. The organisation of horticultural societies: in examining excellent specimens of vegetables and learning how these might best be cultivated those attempting reform were sure that 'pleasurable emotions will be engendered and fostered, lessons of lasting importance will be learned, and high moral sentiment will be imbibed'.[27] Sometimes rational entertainments could be combined, as at the magnificent annual horticultural shows held on Castle Green. At the second of these, in July 1851, a 'large assemblage of elegantly-dressed and fashionable company' wandered round the four tents looking at flowers arranged 'with great taste and judgment' in one, fruit and vegetables in a second, and cottagers' contributions in a third. And then, perhaps while sampling

the ices and delicacies of the season in the fourth tent, they could listen to the band of the 82nd Regiment, which was in attendance by kind permission of Lieutenant-Colonel Maxwell, and which, at intervals, 'discoursed sweet music in a most masterly manner'. In the evening the indefatigable Committee of the *fête champêtre* organised a concert in the Shirehall. There was the band again, but now the singers from the cathedral too. And the Shirehall was 'filled by a highly respectable, intelligent, and fashionable audience, and, being brilliantly lighted … [there was] revealed to our view an array of intellectual countenances beaming with pleasure and animation, and presenting a scene of the most gratifying description'.

The music was judiciously selected and the band displayed their taste and thorough training in their 'chaste' executions. There were doubts about the acoustics of the Shirehall for the band, that they would be less advantageous than the greensward, but in fact the sound was 'perfectly electrical'. The vocal offerings were, naturally, 'of a reposo character'. The first glee, Thomas Cooke's *Strike the lyre* was, quite understandably, 'given with a little nervous feeling (though with much sweetness), which however was soon removed by the cheering plaudits of the audience'. And then glees by Müller and Spofforth and Bishop's exquisite serenade *Sleep, gentle lady*. This was 'rational entertainment'. The receipts were very satisfactory too, the Hereford Journal reported.[28]

The earliest performances of the Choral Society

Who sang in the Choral Society in these earliest years? There appear to be no records, no names of singers who can be identified. Twenty years later though – with the aims and objects of the Society unchanged – four members of the Society (four of the 'most respectable' members) sang as supernumeraries on Sundays in the cathedral choir. One was a watchmaker, one of the others a wheelwright, one a hatter, one a clockmaker.[29] And it was boys who sang the top line with the men of the Choral Society. Of the names which can be identified during these early years, they seem to be boys who were choristers in the cathedral choir. Perhaps there were additional boys as well.

What did they sing? They sang the 'Hallelujah Chorus' at the opening of St Peter's Sunday-school in June 1838.[30] In July they sang during the celebrations to mark the coronation of Queen Victoria. This was during a lecture by the Vicar of St Peter's on coronation ceremonies and their significance, and their singing of the sixteenth-century Latin hymn, *Non nobis, Domine*, 'afforded high gratification'.[31] In October 1838 the Choral Society sang at a morning service in All Saints' Church held annually whose pur-

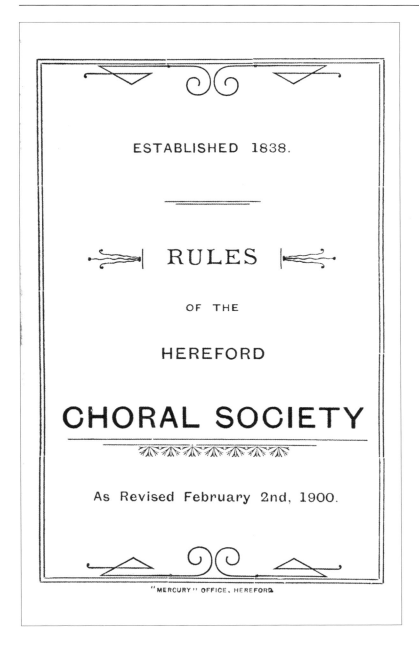

ESTABLISHED 1838.

RULES

OF THE

HEREFORD

CHORAL SOCIETY

As Revised February 2nd, 1900.

"MERCURY" OFFICE, HEREFORD.

I.—The object of the Society shall be the Cultivation of SACRED and SECULAR MUSIC, both Vocal and Instrumental, and also the formation of a body of persons capable of assisting at the Triennial Musical Festivals of Hereford, Gloucester, and Worcester.

II.—The Honorary Officers of the Society shall be as follows:—Conductor, the Organist of the Cathedral; Treasurer and two Secretaries, all of whom shall be appointed by the Society in General Meeting.

III.—The general affairs of the Society shall be managed by a Committee of gentlemen, consisting of the Honorary Officers, the Mayor of Hereford, and twelve Members of the Society elected at a General Meeting, six of whom shall retire each year, but be eligible for re-election.

IV.—The Librarian shall have sole charge of the Music, and be responsible for the proper care of the same.

The Secretary shall keep a register of the Attendance of Members and Minutes of General and Special Meetings. He shall also keep a Balance Sheet of Members' Fees and Subscriptions.

V.—Persons desirous of being admitted into the Society must be proposed and seconded by Members at an Ordinary Practice, and shall satisfy the Conductor as to voice and musical capacity, and shall be elected by the votes of Members (openly or by ballot, as preferred by them), at an ordinary Practice Meeting subsequent to that at which the person was proposed, and after passing the musical test of the Conductor. In the event of a ballot being taken, one black ball in four to exclude.

pose was the raising of funds for the Female National School, an establishment which gave poor girls in Hereford a 'plain and useful education' and sent them forth as 'honest and industrious' domestic servants. On this occasion again they sang the 'Hallelujah Chorus', which 'did infinite credit', it was reported, 'to Mr Hunt and the Members of the Hereford Choral Society'.[32] They were always singing the 'Hallelujah Chorus'.

They sang at this service for the Female National School in subsequent years. In December 1838 some of the members began to assist regularly at an evening service on Sundays at All Saints.[33] In August 1839 they sang a full cathedral service in the Collegiate Church of Bromyard to mark the opening of a new organ built by Mr Walker of Tottenham Court Road, London.[34] They sang with the vicars choral at an annual service in the cathedral for a charity which raised money for the clothing and apprenticing of poor children in Herefordshire.[35] They sang at the laying of the foundation stone for the new church of St Martin's in October 1840, and at a service in October 1841 to raise additional funds for the building.[36] In March 1841 they sang at a service to mark the first anniversary of the Mechanics' Institution and at a *soirée musicale* afterwards.[37] The local papers in these early years document the rising standards achieved by the Society. In the summer of 1840 the *Times* found the Society 'in a very improving state' and thought the members were becoming 'most efficient as chorus singers'.[38] Very early on Christmas Day that year, 'in the still hour of repose', 'the vocal strains' of about twenty members of the Society were heard outside the houses of some of the Patrons and honorary members, giving them 'an agreeable surprise', or at least that's how the *Hereford Journal* described it.[39]

Soon after the choral society had been established John Hunt let it be known that he planned to create 'an instrumental society': choral and instrumental societies would form 'an Institution [to] develop the native musical talent of this city'. The *Hereford Times* saluted this endeavour: 'The great advantage which such an institution will afford to the conductor of our triennial festivals alone, must be at once obvious … Should there be persons desirous of performing on an instrument but whose means are inadequate to the gratification of such desire', still, the paper exhorts its readers, apply to Mr Hunt who 'will be happy to respond to the application.'[40] Whether John Hunt really did have sponsors waiting to assist and buy instruments is not clear. It would have been a very ambitious scheme. The population of Hereford in these years was about 11,000. The potential number of young men who might have the time and inclination to learn a musical instrument must have been very small. At any rate nothing much seems to have come of this initiative.

The Hereford Philharmonic and Choral Societies

But then, on 7 February 1844, the Choral Society took part in a concert of instrumental items, solo songs and choral pieces. It certainly impressed the reporter from the *Hereford Times*: 'We cannot but congratulate the inhabitants of our ancient city upon the possession of such musical talent'.

The instrumental items included four overtures, to Handel's *Atalanta*, to Rossini's *La Gazza Ladra*, Beethoven's *Prometheus* and Auber's *Masaniello*. There were also two symphonies, the 'First Symphony' of both Mozart and Haydn. These were most likely adaptations or arrangements from such publications as *Grand Symphonies by Beethoven, Haydn and Mozart, arranged for the Harp and Piano Forte, with Accompaniments for the Flute and Violoncello* by

N C Bochsa, published in London by Chappells about 1832, or *Haydn's Grand Symphonies Composed for Mr Salomon's concerts, and arranged for five instruments, vizt two violins, a German flute, a tenor and a violoncello: with an accompaniment for the pianoforte, ad libitum* by J P Salomon, published about 1820.

The newspaper critic thought that the Handel offered a very good opportunity to judge the efficiency of the band, and, everyone agreed, the overture was played 'in capital style'. Being a critic, he had to find fault of course, and some of his comments no doubt struck his readers as mere pedantry: he regretted the absence of 'a few wind instruments' in the orchestra, and he'd missed particularly the splendid roll of the drums in *La Gazza Ladra*. But they

---

CHRISTMAS SPECIAL MEETING,

January 21d, 1856.

PROGRAMME:

OVERTURE .... "PASTOR FIDO." ... HANDEL.

MOZART'S FIRST SERVICE.

SOLI—MASTER HEWSON; MESSRS. BURVILL, BARNBY, HERBERT, and T. CARPENTER.

" KYRIE."	" SANCTUS."
" GLORIA."	" BENEDICTUS."
" CREDO."	" AGNUS DEI."

CONCERTO .... HANDEL.
AIR—Mr. BARNBY—" In native worth." (*Creation*.) HAYDN.
QUARTETT AND CHORUS } MASTER HEWSON; MESSRS. BURVILL, BARNBY, and T. CARPENTER—" Be peace on earth." (*Palestine*.) .. CROTCH.
AIR—Mr. HERBERT—" If with all your hearts." (*Elijah*.) .... MENDELSSOHN.
CHORALE—" To God on high." (*St. Paul*.) .. „
AIR—Mr. BURVILL—" Softly rise." (*Solomon*.).. DR. BOYCE.
CHORUS—" O! Father." (*Judas Maccabæus*.).. HANDEL.
AIR—Mr. T. CARPENTER—" Arm, ye brave." .... „
CHORUS—" We come." .... „

It is requested that the Audience will abstain from censure or applause.

G. TOWNSHEND SMITH, HON. DIRECTOR.

hadn't got any clarinets. Or any drums. An octave roll on the piano was not quite the same thing, no doubt. Maybe not, but there could only be drums during the Choral Meetings in the summer, during the Three Choirs Festivals. On the whole the musical critic from the *Hereford Times* was extremely complimentary. By the end of the concert the performers seemed to have lost any little nervousness apparent at the commencement of the concert, and were giving 'most spirited and clever performances'. It all augured well; if the band could handle so difficult a piece as Mozart's 'First Symphony' already, what might be expected of them after a few more months' practice together?

Mr Townshend Smith, the new organist of Hereford Cathedral, delighted the company when he presented his own song, a 'Vocal Rondo', *The wild rose*. Members of the Choral Society presented two glees, Danby's *When Sappho tun'd the quiv'ring lyre* and Horsley's *By Celia's Arbour,* given 'very creditably' according to the *Times*. With new ventures like this, you had to be tolerant, and it was true, the Choral Society's rendering of *By Celia's Arbour* was sung 'very flat throughout, in spite of Mr Smith's efforts to keep them in tune'. But the *Times* critic ended his review on a positive note: 'we take our leave wishing with all our heart prosperity to the Society', he smiled encouragingly, 'looking forward with confidence to a similar treat in March next, when the second concert takes place'.[41]

But where did these instrumentalists come from? The reviewer writes of the Choral Society but the review is headed 'Hereford Philharmonic Society'. What had happened? There had been a merger, or a pact, or at least an understanding with another fledgling organisation. What was the Hereford Philharmonic Society?

In the early eighteenth century members of the College of Vicars Choral would meet one evening each week for music, ale, cider and tobacco. Fifteen or sixteen of those attending would be designated performers, and seven or eight non-performers. And all members could introduce friends as visitors. To act as leader the little band turned to Thomas Woodcock, who kept a coffee-house and was a most excellent violinist. He played the solos of Signor Corelli with such exquisite neatness and elegance. And to him the vicars choral gave five shillings each evening they met.[42] How long this congenial arrangement lasted, and why it stopped is not recorded. Perhaps it lapsed from time to time and was periodically revived during the eighteenth century. At any rate on 1 February 1836 a little group of mostly middle-aged men, the vicars choral and their friends, met in the College with the object of creating something similar, establishing 'a Philharmonic Club vocal and instrumental'. From the first week in October to the last week in March they would meet in the Common Room of the Vicars' College, they decided.[43] Yes,

it would be possible in the winter now, with those new gas lights in every street. Everyone would assemble at a quarter to seven and between seven and half past nine they would make music together. And then they would take refreshments, a dish of cold meat, bread and cheese, and some beer, cider, brandy and wine. Later on in the autumn at another meeting it was proposed and agreed upon – though surely not without one or two raised eyebrows – that it might be sensible if a pot of tea were also provided. They would finish at eleven punctually.

Who was there on that February evening in 1836? Who were these vicars choral and their cronies? There was Christopher Jones, born in 1781, who'd been a chorister at Hereford, and had had harpsichord lessons with Mr Pearce, the deputy organist at the cathedral. He'd been a pupil at the Cathedral School though he'd received additional coaching from Mr Picard, himself a vicar choral, in his rooms in the College. He had taken a degree at Christ Church, Oxford and returned as a vicar choral in January 1806. And Edward Howells there, born in 1886, he did the same, a Hereford chorister, a pupil at the Cathedral School, his degree at Christ Church and an appointment as vicar choral at Hereford. And The Revd Munsey, William Munsey. He was elected in the same year, 1810, as a vicar choral. He was the son of James Munsey, who had the Crown and Sceptre in Widemarsh Street for years and years. Somehow Old Munsey must have had some money. They all thought William had dropped out, leaving All Souls like that. But he'd transferred to Trinity Hall, Cambridge and did graduate in the end.[44]

There was young John Hunt, the new organist, who'd arrived only three months earlier, still in his twenties. What an impression he was making, so enthusiastic and talented. Such devotional organ playing, as you'd expect from such a nice unostentatious young man. And with a most beautiful counter-tenor voice. Of course that was discovered by an old Hereford vicar choral, William Cooke, the Vicar of Bromyard. It was in Salisbury, at a musical party at the house of Mr Corfe, the cathedral organist, and John Hunt was singing bass as he usually did. A fine voice. And then Webbe's *When winds breathe soft* came up. Exquisite! And they needed a countertenor. Well, Mr Cooke asked young Hunt if he could sing the countertenor part. 'I've never sung this part before', Hunt replied. 'I've never sung countertenor before.' Off he went and found another room with a piano in it and he tried it over by himself and then came back. It was a great surprise to the assembled company and a great surprise too to Mr Hunt. And that was the beginning of his career as a countertenor. Of course he'd been a lay clerk at Lichfield in recent years. But his grounding had been with the admirable Arthur Corfe at Salisbury, as a chorister and then as an apprentice.[45]

What about the instrumentalists of the Philharmonic Club? They had Mr Hunt as a keyboard player. And fortunately, The Revd Christopher Jones, as well as being an excellent keyboard player himself, was a violinist. A most useful musician, The Revd Jones. He certainly had, as someone put it, 'a practical knowledge of choral duty', but with his excellent high tenor voice he also delighted everyone in the College when he sang songs to his own piano accompaniment.[46] They had a dependable flute in Francis Merewether, the Rector of Woolhope and brother of the Dean.

Two or three of the laymen too seem to have had musical talents. Marcellus Newton, the magistrate, was a violinist. Mr Spozzi, Charles Spozzi, who was at Hoskin & Morgans bank in St Peter's Street, was a viola-player. (Surely he had Italian blood in him, Mr Spozzi, being a fiddle-player like that.)

The non-singing men seemed mostly to be lawyers: there were the Gough brothers, Thomas and Jonathan, Clerk of the Lieutenancy. There was Mr Anderson in St Owen Street. There was Mr Bellamey with his offices in Widemarsh Street and in the Close, treasurer of the Mechanics Institution. Most distinguished of all there was Francis Bodenham, treasurer of the county and commissioner for taking 'Acknowledgements of Deeds by Married Women'. The Bodenhams were a wealthy Catholic family of bankers and solicitors with their country house and estate at Rotherwas, and Francis would serve twice as mayor of the city. No records of the works selected at their earliest weekly meetings seem to have survived. But they surely sang pieces copied from the bound volumes that Christopher Jones presented to the Club in 1838, *Convito Armonico, A Collection of Madrigals, Elegies, Glees, Canons, Catches, and Duets Selected from the Works of the Most Eminent Composers*. Most beautiful volumes, recently published by Chappell's in New Bond Street.[47]

There were madrigals like Dr Dowland's *Come again sweet love*, Mr Thomas Morley's *Now is the month of maying*, Mr Thomas Ford's *Since first I saw your face*, and of course there was Mr Gibbons's *The Silver Swan*. And the candles burned low. Perhaps, like Thomas Hardy, the greybeards oft times wished their hearts had shrunk as thin as their wasting skin. But they hadn't. And they sang of Celia and a voice somewhere was marked with an uncharacteristic vibrato, with throbbings of noontide.

In Celia's face a question did arise
Which were more beautiful, her lips or eyes?

But then, in 1844, the Philharmonic Club, now calling itself the Philharmonic Society – it may have changed its name as early as 1838 – redrafted the rules and issued them in printed form. The So-ciety had raised its ambitions. The stated objects of the Society now, as they were formulated in these new rules, were 'the advancement of Instrumental and Vocal Music in the City and County of Hereford'. The members were to meet every Wednesday evening from October to May at the College Hall. And there were to be special meetings, concerts for the subscribers and also open to the public, provided members of the audiences realised that they would be expected to behave themselves: 'No conversation during the performance of the music', was one of the Society's rules. There would be 'competent performing members', proposed and seconded by two members, and approved of by the stewards and director, and also 'persons willing to promote the object of this Society' who could become subscribers by the annual payment of five shillings due on 1 January. The Patrons of the Philharmonic Society included the Bishop of Hereford, the Lord-Lieutenant of the County and five local members of Parliament, and the President was Dean Merewether. There was a printed list of 127 subscribing members in 1844.[48]

And what of the new non-performing members, the subscribers who had joined since 1837? There were even more lawyers. There was William Aston in St Peter Street. There was Thomas Evans with his offices in the cathedral close, solicitor, proctor, Notary Public, Coroner of the County of Hereford, secretary to the Lord Bishop of Hereford. Several of the solicitors and bankers also acted as insurance agents, men like Thomas Hardwick in Broad Street, who was the fire and life assurance agent for Britannia Life. There was Richard Johnson with his solicitor's offices in St Owen Street, also Clerk of the Peace for the city, registrar to the Archdeacon of Salop and agent for Clerical, Medical and General Life. There were teachers: Mr Joseph Evans in Berrington Street and Mr James Weymss in Widemarsh Street Without with their Gentlemen's Boarding Schools. There were doctors, Dr Glasspoole and Captain Price, the surgeon, of St Owen's Street. There were the men of commerce: Mr Ebenezer Child, of High Street, the 'Music and Musical Instrument Seller', Mr Morse, of High Town, the 'Chemist and Druggist', Mr William Vale, also in High Town, 'Printer, Bookseller, Bookbinder, Stationer and Printseller'. There was Mr Ververs, of High Town, 'Ironmonger, Manufacturer of Tin, Iron and Copper Goods'. And just a few ladies became subscribers: Lady Peyton, Mrs Gethen – still keeping her late husband's drapery business going and the funeral side of it as well. And Miss James, too. Which Miss James would that be? Margaret, the shopkeeper and maltster in Eign Street? Well, probably Miss James in Castle Street, who runs the 'Boarding School for Ladies'. And Mrs Williams too. But which Mrs Williams? Jane, in St Peter's Street, the straw-hat maker? No, it must be Theodosia who comes all the way from Ross, from *her*

HEREFORD CHORAL SOCIETY.

EASTER SPECIAL MEETING
APRIL 15, 1857.

PROGRAMME.

PART 1.

OVERTURE—Esther ....*Handel.*
MOZART'S FIRST SERVICE.
SOLI—*Masters Bayliss and Payne, Messrs. Dyson, Barnby and Bradley.*
CHORUS AND DUET—" Kyrie eleison."
CHORUS AND QUARTETT—" Gloria in Excelsis."
CHORUS AND QUARTETT—" Credo."
CHORUS—" Sanctus."
QUARTETT—" Benedictus."
CHORUS—" Hosanna !"
SOLO—" Agnus dei."
DUET AND CHORUS—" Dona nobis."

PART 2.

OVERTURE—(Occasional Oratorio) ....*Handel.*
AIR—Mr. BRADLEY.." O God have mercy,"..St. Paul ....*Mendelssohn.*
CHORALE—"To God on high."   „   „
AIR—Mr. HERBERT.." Be thou faithful,"   „   „
CHORUS—" Come gentle Spring" ....(Seasons).........*Haydn.*
SONG—Mr. T. CARPENTER.." With joy"   „   „
CHORUS AND QUARTETT—" Marv'lous"   „   „
AIR—Mr. BURVILL.." O magnify the Lord"................*Handel.*
QUARTETT & CHORUS—" Blest are the Departed"..(Last
      Judgment) ....*Spohr.*
AIR—Mr DYSON—"Thou shalt bring them in"..(Israel in Egypt) *Handel.*
EASTER HYMN—" Jesus Christ is Risen" ....*Dr. Worgan.*
AIR—Mr. BARNBY.." Then shall the Righteous"..(Elijah) *Mendelssohn*
GRAND CHORUS—" Hallelujah"..(Messiah) ....*Handel.*

It is requested that the Audience will not applaud or censure.

G. TOWNSHEND SMITH, *Hon. Director.*

This was the little music club that the vicars choral had managed to establish. They saw themselves – and nobody would dream of contradicting them – as the musical experts. Perhaps they did manage to encourage a few more of the laymen to join in a glee. Perhaps Mr Anthony was game; perhaps he did have musical talent which the eulogists omitted in enumerating all his gifts and achievements. He founded the *Hereford Times*, he was mayor of the city six times, he led the renaming of the city's key streets, oversaw the installation of the first iron bridge over the Wye at Hunderton, the creation of a new drainage system, the building of Barrs Court railway station. He was the man who piloted through a scheme for a new cattle market, and presided over the opening of the butter, poultry and meat markets, and established schools. Perhaps he was in fact the possessor of a noble baritone and a consummate sight-reader. It might have been that those who paid tribute to this much loved citizen did not wish to sully his reputation by reference to his unfortunate habit of violin-playing. In 1846 a famous singing teacher who had travelled the length and breadth of England hearing men, women and children sing and had been appointed Professor of Vocal Music at King's College, London in 1844, declared that an 'educated man's singing must create surprise, if no pleasure'.[49] At any rate we can be sure that most of the prominent male citizens of Hereford in the middle of the nineteenth century could not read music, could not sing, could not play an instrument and had no wish at all to join a choir. But they could forgive the eccentricities of their music-loving friends.

The gentlemen of Hereford seem to have had in mind something like the Bath Harmonic Society, which had been in existence longer than anyone could remember. The gentlemen in Bath sought 'innocent and refined enjoyments'. They hoped that 'Delicacy, Moderation, and Respectability would ever continue to be the Distinguishing Characteristics of the Harmonic Society'. And in order to promote harmony 'no political discussion' at meetings was allowed and 'no indecent song or sentiment' could be sung or spoken. No person was eligible into the Bath Harmonic Society but 'noblemen, gentlemen and professional men'. That's how they put it in words in their rules, which were included in *A selection of Favourite Catches, Glees, &c as sung at the Bath Harmonic Society*, published in 1799.[50] Such a society was as much for friendship and fellowship as music. It was also for networking.

Number seventeen of that new printed list of rules that appeared early in 1844 stated: 'This Society will assist the Choral Society at their Special Meetings.' So, from now on, members of the Philharmonic formed the band for the Choral Society. The young men 'from the humbler classes' now made music with the middle-class

'Boarding School for Ladies'. They're *so* musical, those headmistresses. Most of the subscribers were from Hereford itself but there were indeed a few who would have had to travel far, like Theodosia, on very muddy roads. Dr Rootes, the surgeon, was also from Ross and Nathaniel Morgan too of the Ross *&* Archenfield Bank. And Captain Harris all the way from Kington, the honorary actuary for the savings bank there.

clergymen and their friends. The Choral Society continued to sing at least occasionally at special services by itself. It certainly sang for several years at the annual service for the Diocesan SPCK and the Propagation of the Gospel in Foreign Parts. In 1844 and in 1845 a 'full cathedral service' was advertised.

The Philharmonic continued with its own series too; both Societies seemed to aim at four 'special meetings' each year. The Philharmonic would include songs and solo instrumental pieces, glees and even overtures or symphonies. It would play the 'First Symphony' of Mozart or the 'First' of Beethoven or the 'Third' of Haydn, arrangements or adaptations of arrangements. The orchestra which played 'Mozart's First Symphony' in February 1844 – 'not yet in its full strength', the *Times* reported – consisted of the six violins, two violas, three cellos, two double-basses and two flutes.[51] The Choral Society naturally gave pride of place in their programmes to choruses. They wouldn't sing a complete oratorio. They sang 'selections'.

The Easter Special Meeting in 1845 was an all-Handel programme: the first half opened with the overture to *Solomon* followed by the second part of *Messiah*, and the second part opened with the overture to *Alexander's Feast* followed by the third part of *Messiah*. Or the programme might be much more of a miscellany: a Handel overture and the *Dettingen Te Deum* in the first half, another Handel overture to begin the second half, a chorus from *Judas Maccabaeus*, a quartet and chorus from Crotch's *Palestine*, William Croft's anthem *God is gone up*, solos and choruses from *The Creation* of Haydn, and ending with a chorus from *Samson*. How were these concerts received? Like everybody else, the man from the *Hereford Journal* first of all examined the audience and was often impressed by 'a numerous and fashionable assembly'. Even on those occasions when attendance was by no means as numerous as it ought to have been, the man from the *Hereford Journal* was at least gratified that 'it was highly respectable'.[52] With the band came its subscribers: the Choral Society was now being brought to the attention of men and women who wished to come to concerts and were financially easily able to do so.

At the Easter concert in 1844 the critic noticed hesitation and indecision in the playing and singing at the beginning of the concert but did not wish to do more than allude to this, 'a very usual fault with young societies'. Miss Cole gave 'I know that my Redeemer liveth' very creditably. Members of the chorus took solos too – Master Hill, one of the cathedral choristers, sang 'very chastely'. Mr Carpenter, it had to be said, was generally 'a *little* too *staccato*'. He must choose his arias carefully to suit his style.[53] The Whitsuntide concert that year, the reporter thought, 'afforded high gratification

to the auditory, which comprised most of the leading families of the city'. Selections from *The Creation* were performed, with Mr Harris singing 'very prettily'; Mr Garland gave the recitative and air, 'And God said, let the waters', in a manner 'which elicited the approbation of some experienced amateurs capable of forming an accurate judgment'. The *Journal* considered the choruses accurately sung, especially 'The Heavens are telling'. This piece though did tend to quicken up and towards the end it became just too fast. There was also 'a very observable weakness' in the alto and bass parts.[54]

HEREFORD CHORAL SOCIETY

MIDSUMMER SPECIAL MEETING.
JUNE 9th, 1858.

OVERTURE—"La Clemenza di Tito "......*Mozart.*
MADRIGAL—"Now is the Month of Maying "...*Morley.*
PRIZE GLEE—" Ye Nightingales "......*A. Montem Smith.*
PART SONG—" Awake sweet Love "......*Dowland.*
SERENADE—Mr. HERBERT—"The Brook is purling "...*Bartholomew.*
PART SONG—" Dulce Domum "......*Reading.*
SOLO VIOLIN—Mr. PRITCHARD—Fantasia from " Il Trovatore "......*Verdi.*
GLEE—" Strike the Lyre ".........*T. Cooke.*
ANTE-MADRIGAL—"Who shall win my lady fair" *Pearsall.*
BALLAD—Mr. T. CARPENTER—"If loved by thee" *Wallace.*
PART SONG—" O who will o'er the downs "...*Pearsall.*

OVERTURE—" Tancredi ".........*Rossini.*
PART SONG—" The Pedlar ".........*Dowland.*
SONG—Mr. BARNBY—"Ye Sons of Merry England" *Perring.*
MADRIGAL—" I saw lovely Phillis "......*Pearsall.*
GLEE—" Soldier's Song ".........*Werner.*
ANDANTE AND MINUET—*Haydn.*
PART SONG—" The Hardy Norseman "......*Pearsall.*
MADRIGAL—" We happy Shepherd Swains " *Nethercliffe.*
GLEE, WITH CHORUS—" O bold Robin Hood "...*Sir H. R. Bishop.*

G. TOWNSHEND SMITH,
Hon. Director.

Who was this soprano soloist, Miss Cole, who sang with the Choral Society on several occasions? The Misses Cole, Susanna and Charlotte, were born at Tarrington, where their father taught music and was organist of the parish church. They both studied at the Royal Academy of Music under Manuel Garcia, and both had successful careers, at one time as The Misses Cole, specialising in singing duets together. Their London debut was at Exeter Hall in 1849. Their brother, James, was a treble in the cathedral choir and while he was still a chorister wrote a number of services and even an oratorio, *Deborah and Barpak*.[55]

In February 1846 the Society announced a 'Concert of Sacred Music' with the specific purpose of raising funds. They couldn't pay their bills for some stoves they'd purchased nor for some music they'd bought.[56] The concert designed to help them out of this tricky situation was a decided musical success: the man from the *Hereford Times* reported that the way the Benedictus from Mozart's *Requiem* was sung was 'felt to be beautiful by the entire audience'. And the way the overture from *The Last Judgement* was played by this amateur orchestra 'would have elicited a plaudit from Spohr himself'. Unfortunately though, the company was not very large.[57] At any rate, it was possible for the Society to hold its Easter Special Meeting and the concert at Whitsuntide too, at which, besides a number of new pieces, the auditory were able to enjoy again the Benedictus from Mozart's *Requiem* and the Spohr overture.

And then in August readers of the *Journal* were reassured that the Choral Society were working hard at Spohr's *The Fall of Babylon* for the Three Choirs Festival in September and that 'everything betokens an excellent meeting'. It reminded them that, after being closed for six years, 'the nave of that sacred and spacious edifice … will again re-echo with the sublime and inspiring strains'.[58]

And apparently it did. The critic for the *London Standard*, however, thought he should try to explain that the 'chromatic form of expression which belongs so peculiarly to Spohr' is not to be mastered immediately by a '"triple provincial choir" that comes into union at long intervals'. Even he, though, did find a few compliments while artfully managing to qualify all of them: 'But there was much to commend even on the score of discipline; and some of the choruses, little short of sublime in their largeness both of form and purpose, came out with surprising amplitude and effect – recollecting the comparative paucity of the numbers'.[59]

The Choral Society silenced

But then the special meetings at least – the Society's public concerts – seem to have ceased. Representatives of the Hereford Choral Society are listed in the publicity for the 1847 Three Choirs Festival at Gloucester, so their own meetings for rehearsal presumably continued. A meeting of the members in April 1848 was reported with the statement that it was 'very probable' that concerts would be resumed within a few months'[60] though the Society wasn't mentioned at the 1848 festival and it seems that concerts were in fact not resumed.

There was no mention of the Society even at the Hereford festival in 1849. It is included among the choirs at Gloucester in 1850, but it appears that the Society itself gave no concerts that year, nor indeed in 1851. But in June 1851, the *Hereford Journal* did announce that, 'after remaining dormant for so long a time, the Hereford Choral Society is about to be revived.'[61] There had been several attempts to re-start, the *Journal* explained, but all had failed. The auguries looked much more favourable now with the appointment of six new lay clerks in the cathedral. In October though, there were still too few subscriptions to begin. It was not until March 1852 that the paper could announce that regular Monday meetings would resume, 'these agreeable *réunions*'.[62]

The first concert of the newly constituted chorus was the Whitsuntide Special Meeting on 1 June 1852, and the *Journal* was very pleased to see 'so fashionable and numerous an assemblage at the rational and musical treat provided'. The choir sang selections from Handel's *Judas Maccabaeus*, *Samson*, and *The Creation*, 'with two Overtures for the instrumentals'. 'The performers, both instrumental and vocal, acquitted themselves most charmingly', in the opinion of the *Hereford Journal* reporter, and, 'but for the regulations usually adopted at concerts of sacred music, much and deserved applause would have been elicited.'[63]

From the start it was clear that the new lay clerks, appointed in March 1851, were crucial to the success of the new undertaking. They sang as members of the chorus but they also sang solos, rendered, as the *Journal* put it, 'with taste and much feeling'. Perhaps they were given some kind of fee, but this was surely much less than a specially engaged soloist would have required. The occasion was clearly a great success and augured well for the future of 'this agreeable Society', 'this useful Society', as the paper was now describing it. 'Mr G T Smith, our kind and invaluable organist of the Cathedral, conducted with his usual good taste, skill, and courtesy, and the company separated about half-past ten, much delighted with the evening's arrangements and entertainment.'[64] Its concert in October 1854 attracted 'a large and respectable audience' for its performance of 'Mozart's 12th Mass', long misattributed in the nineteenth century and really by a Viennese composer of light operas called Wenzel Müller. The choruses were 'careful and telling' and sung 'with neatness and expression' even though the chorus

HEREFORD

CHORAL SOCIETY.

THE MIDSUMMER

SPECIAL MEETING

WILL BE HELD

IN THE COLLEGE HALL,

(By permission of the Custos and Vicars,)

ON WEDNESDAY EVENING, JUNE 15TH, 1870,

COMMENCING AT 8 O'CLOCK PRECISELY;

WHEN A SELECTION OF

MADRIGALS, PART-SONGS, SONGS,

AND

INSTRUMENTAL MUSIC,

WILL BE PERFORMED.

Tickets may be obtained of Mr. ROBERT CARPENTER, and of the
BOOK AND MUSIC SELLERS.

ADMISSION TO NON-SUBSCRIBERS:

FRONT SEATS, 2s. 6d.; BACK SEATS, 1s.

The Subscription for Non-performing Members is as follows :—
Single Subscription, to entitle the Subscriber to one non-transferable
ticket for all Concerts in the year, 5/. per annum ; Double Subscription,
to admit two persons of the same family, 7/6 per annum ; Family Subscription to admit not more than four, 10/. per annum; School Subscription, 5/. Principal, and 2/6 for each Pupil. The Subscription to be
payable on the first of January in each year.

*Subscribers' Names to be forwarded to Mr. R. Carpenter, Academy,
Saint Owen's Street.*

At the Easter and Christmas Special Meetings, Sacred Music is
performed. Concerts, consisting of Cantatas, Glees, Madrigals, Part
Songs, &c., are given at Midsummer and Michaelmas.

was 'rather deficient in trebles'.[65] At the Easter *soirée musicale* in 1855 Mendelssohn's *Lobegesang* was 'very cleverly given', and the fashionable audience were 'highly gratified' with the singing.[66]

The Musical Times had noted that at the 1855 Three Choirs Festival at Hereford there was a higher proportion of 'professional musicians' than ever before, more professionals among the band, presumably. Perhaps he also meant to signify better voices among the visiting chorus singers. He explained that the organisers were now aware of more visitors coming not just from the adjoining counties, but from further afield by railway, which was encouraging them to aspire to the highest standards possible.[67] At any rate from 1856 there's a shift in tone in the writing of the anonymous reviewer on the *Hereford Times*. The writing becomes more critical and a note of condescension enters. He wishes now to assess and make judgments, not to celebrate the achievements of his own community. Is this a new writer? Is this a young critic determined to demonstrate his sophistication? Perhaps the same reporter has himself taken advantage of railway travel to gain wider experience, and now returns to Hereford which feels, nay, which is – one cannot avoid saying it – rather … well, provincial. He likes to say, 'of course'. And his sentences now tend to be rather long. And he must slip in the names of those masters of vocal interpretation of whom he is undoubtedly a connoisseur.

'Of course among the members of local societies like these one cannot expect to find the highest order of talent; we should not set such store on Grisi, Mario, Novello, or Reeves if they belonged to a common class: but to say that a programme like the one below was well performed throughout by the unaided forces of the Hereford Choral and Philharmonic Societies, is not a little to their praise, especially when we recollect that by a large majority of those members, "the heavenly art" is pursued merely as a recreation from terrestrial and everyday pursuits'. The critic did, however, single out the rich voice of Mr Bradley and a glee called *Ye nightingales* written by Montem Smith, a lay clerk at Westminster Abbey and the conductor's brother, which received a performance that certainly did justice to its merits.[68]

And then came the Society's summer concert of 1858. Here everything and everyone came in for stinging criticism except the conductor. Even the advertising. On the evening of Wednesday 9 June it was Society's Special Midsummer Meeting in College Hall – 'which, by the way, nobody seemed to know anything about.' Those whom any self-respecting town looks to for support and patronage in the cultural sphere, the writer reported, were almost entirely absent. He means what he would characterise as the professional educated classes. Were there twenty of them? The whole dingy business failed to meet the expectations of a cathedral city. 'The room was as bare and wretched-looking as a charity-school, or a poverty-stricken mechanic's [sic] institute; the corps, instrumental and vocal, [exhibited] abundant zeal and energy, with practised capability in an inverse ratio.' Having Mr Townshend Smith as director guaranteed that the orchestra could play the notes in time. But where was the light and shade? Where was the presentation of the composer's unfolding argument? Either there was simply not enough 'local capability, professional and dilettanti', or there was a lack of 'sympathising appreciation' from the musical public. 'Save to those who, guided by recent and pretty unvarying experience, went expecting nothing, the concert was a disappointment'.[69]

In the concert in July 1861 the reviewer makes no particular comment on the boys' voices, simply venturing to remark that the singing would be much improved by the introduction of women's voices.[70] In the Michaelmas Special Meeting in October 1861 he simply observes that the short-comings of the trebles were too obvious to be overlooked. He was very glad to hear that female voices were to be recruited. The Haydn Symphony in E flat, 'rendered with great ease and neatness', the reviewer considered the high point of the evening. Mr Carpenter sang Mr Samuel Lover's *The Two Barrels* – the Englishman has his barrel of beer in the house but he also has his rifle: 'So tankards and rifles let's charge, hip hurra!/ For our Freedom, our Country, and Queen!' Mr Carpenter did sing it well. But he was rewarded, 'after the style usual with music-lovers', with an encore. So he repeated it, which meant that a programme that ought to have been shorter became even longer.[71]

Perhaps the *Hereford Times'* hand-wringing over lack of public support had had an effect, for the first detail that the reviewer noted at the concert in February 1862 was that a 'great many of the élite of the town and county were present'. The earlier choruses from Crotch's *Palestine* were sung tamely but things improved. 'Lo! Starled Chiefs' was splendidly performed, and by the band too in a specially-made arrangement by Mr Townshend Smith. And in Master Martin the choir had a good treble soloist who sang very nicely in the Agnus Dei of Mozart's Mass in C.[72]

In College Hall on 4 September 1863 there was a presentation by members of the Society to their conductor. Mr Phillips, the bookseller in High Town, had made 'chaste gilt frames' for 'four beautiful specimens of the photographic art', pictures taken of portraits of Handel, Haydn, Beethoven, and Mozart. There was also a very elegant time-piece with elaborate workmanship from a design by Mr Bezant – the jeweller in Widemarsh Street, a member of the Society – of the kind known as English skeleton, of Gothic pattern, with turrets and crosses, and pierced framework, and it struck a deep note in imitation of the cathedral bell. And Mr Carpenter, the organist at All Saints, the secretary of the Society and one of the cathedral lay-clerks, read an address and expressed the members' gratitude to Mr Smith for all the help he had given them – these enthusiastic but rather rough amateurs, he conceded – in improving their musical taste and raising their musical skills. And Mr Carpenter thanked Mr Smith too for his unfailing kindness and courtesy at all their meetings. On the front of the time-piece was a lyre and on that was inscribed: 'Presented to G Townshend Smith Esq, by the members of the Hereford Choral Society, as a token of their high esteem for his untiring zeal as honorary director'. And they dated it 'January 1st 1863'. They did this now not because Mr Smith was

leaving – they wished him many years of happiness and prosperity and many more years wielding the baton in front of them – but because they considered an era had ended. They talked of an 'extension' of the Choral Society.[73]

In their Spring Special Meeting they had sung 'Spring' of Haydn's *The Seasons* with just trebles on the top line. But in their Summer Special Meeting of 22 July 1863, the Hereford Choral Society sang 'Autumn' from *The Seasons* with the cathedral trebles and the forty-nine gentlemen joined now by twenty-one ladies.[74]

An 'altogether amateur' Society

As the *Hereford Times* explained to its readers: 'By the exertions of the friends and promoters of the society, a number of ladies of musical talent living in the city and neighbourhood were secured for the feminine parts, thus giving the society the character of an altogether amateur one, and what is far more important, cultivating a taste for the study of music in its most refined branches.' In this first concert of the new dispensation there was a soprano soloist; it isn't made clear whether she was a chorus member or not. There was also a treble soloist. The soloists in the three lower parts are lay clerks.

The Choral Society retained the cathedral's trebles but it's not clear how many sang in subsequent years, nor whether they habitually sang. At the Annual Meeting on New Year's Day 1892 it was noted that there were too few men singing, but a strong soprano line and the cathedral choristers in addition. Sinclair thought that it would be better to drop the boys. When this was done is unclear. At any rate it was suggested that they be brought back in 1919 in the difficult conditions immediately after the war.

But the singing of the chorus on this occasion in 1863 was 'refined and cultivated'. The three lay clerks who sang as soloists were firm favourites with Hereford audiences, and the solo treble sang most skilfully, with a particularly sweet tone. He had clearly been most carefully trained. The Society also drew on the services of a professional soprano as a soloist, as they had done in their concerts in the 1840s. This time it was Miss Broad. Perhaps this was Mrs Haynes, the wife of the organist of Malvern Priory. Elizabeth Broad had been trained in London at the Royal Academy of Music and at the Paris Conservatoire.[75] At any rate her 'simple graceful style of singing was much admired'; Miss Broad's voice was 'not powerful, but very sweet, particularly in the higher notes, the lower ones being rather unequal, but very pure and clear'. Perhaps the high point of the evening was a gem of a composition, the reporter from the paper thought, a composition by the up-and-coming Mr Joseph Barnby, a brother of another up-and-coming musician, Mr James Barnby, the

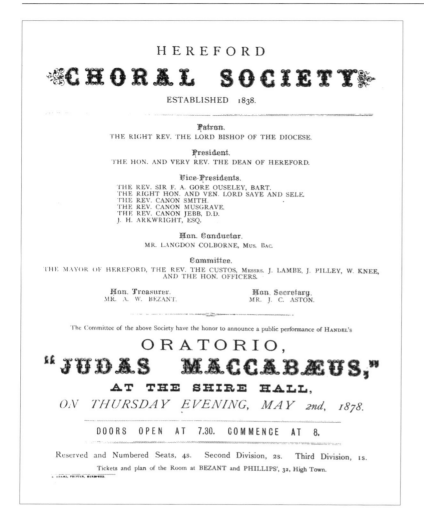

the new dispensation, on 6 October 1863, Hereford experienced the strongest earthquake it had ever felt.[78]

Who was singing in the Choral Society when it became this large choir of men and women? There were professional men like Mr Barker, the architect, with his offices in St Owen Street and in London in Russell Square. There was Stephen Broad, the auctioneer and estate agent in Broad St. There was Mr Lambe, a solicitor and agent to the Provincial Fire and Life Insurance Company, with his wife and daughter. There were tradesmen like Aaron Bezant, the watch and clock maker, and silversmith, in Widemarsh Street; Charles Grizelle, boot and shoe maker, and sexton of the cemetery on Broomy Hill; George Price, jeweller and watchmaker; Henry Magness, who'd been a brazier and was now an inn-keeper; and John Butler in Commercial Road, the coal merchant and agent for Wells' Wallingford stout. There was Mr Barnby, lay clerk and music teacher; The Revd John Goss, vicar choral and son of Sir John Goss, the organist of St Paul's in London; and The Revd F T Havergal, vicar choral, sub-treasurer, and librarian to the Dean and Chapter. There was The Revd John Capel Hanbury, assistant classical master at the Cathedral School. There was the wife of the conductor, Mrs Smith; the wife of Henry Vevers, the surgeon; and Mrs Watkins, who was in charge of the register office for servants in Commercial Street.[79]

There was, in other words, a wide cross-section of Hereford society. The circumstances in which men and women of different social backgrounds could meet in such an informal and intimate setting were rare in a community whose hierarchical structures tended to imprison its members beneath an icy crust of social terror. We have only to remember Elgar with his 'haunting fear' of social disapproval – 'his father keeps a shop', made in an undertone behind his back, or his departing abruptly at the last minute from a dinner party telling the hostess: 'You will not wish your table to be disgraced by the son of a piano-tuner'.[80] He may have been absurdly hypersensitive to perceived slights but, real or imagined, they certainly arose from a striking characteristic of the milieu into which he was born.

A visitor at a concert given by a singing class in Suffolk in the 1840s noticed how the audience of about two hundred consisted of 'working people, servants and apprentices, but there were also tradespeople, farmers and landowners from the district, clergymen and dissenting ministers and their families, and everyone was dressed in their best clothes'. And when the last piece had been sung at their concerts, admiring listeners and warm and tired musicians would join together and talk agreeably. And never on such occasions did 'the semblance of a violation of decorum cast a shadow upon the pleasure of the evening'. Nor was decorum violated at the close of

cathedral lay clerk and a member of the Choral Society. Altogether the concert was a decided success, and the newspaper hoped that the Society would be supported as it deserved.

This first concert had been very well attended and the auguries were good.[76] The reporter at the presentation to Mr Smith later that year suggested that the gentlemen of the old guard were themselves very pleased with the new Society, thought it all very satisfactory and considered that it would soon be thoroughly worthy of an important English cathedral city.[77] Whether there were any dissenting voices, whether any men were outraged, whether any fathers forbade their wives or their daughters to appear in public, bonnet or no bonnet, and to open their mouths wide, whether any grandmothers threatened to disinherit their impudent music-loving grand-daughters is not recorded. But on the eve of the second concert under

The Revd W D V Duncombe (1832–1925),
a bass in the Society for half a century

the evening, when 'the same persons resumed their common social relations as masters and servants, and employers and employed'.[81] Whether the little town of Bungay in the 1840s was really quite such a haven of peaceful coexistence and a model of community relations as this vignette suggests might be doubted. But the high ambitions of the writer for the singing class or choral society, and the possibility of its influencing behaviour far beyond the musical sphere are not in doubt. It took a little longer in Hereford.

The Choral Society was creating a new social situation, or at least one which men and women rarely experienced. They were attempting to co-operate in a mental and physical endeavour in which it was by no means certain the skills of the gentlemen would outstrip those of the ladies. There is little in the meagre Choral Society papers of the 1860s or '70s which reveals anything of beating hearts and dry lips. There's a glimpse, though, in a piece by a music critic in the *Cheltenham On-looker* in 1856. Just before Christmas Mr and Mrs Marshall held a musical party in the Assembly Rooms, but it was so fashionably attended it felt like a Lansdown drawing-room. Mr Marshall of course taught singing, and among his private pu-

pils were several ladies 'moving in the very first circles of society in Cheltenham, and all highly accomplished'. The critic was present in a personal rather than a professional capacity and did not wish to practise his 'ungentle craft'; but he could say that the choral pieces sung by the two dozen or so ladies were charmingly rendered, on the whole. Most delightful was the 'Chorus of Angels' from Michael Costa's *Eli*. Some young gentlemen were persuaded to join their 'fair companions'. They did not sing so well in tune or so steadily, 'a circumstance, perhaps, not much to be wondered at, seeing by whom they were surrounded, and the distraction which must have resulted from the beaming of so many bright eyes'.[82]

When the boot was on the other foot though, gentlemen were not always particularly chivalrous or kind. In 1889 two or three ladies left the chorus of the Herefordshire Philharmonic Society after some gentlemen behind them had kept up incessant running commentaries about them and made rude remarks on their ineptitude as they stumbled on passages the conductor was asking them to repeat by themselves. The ring-leader apparently was none other than The Revd W D V Duncombe, vicar choral at Hereford Cathedral, sometime Minor Canon de Cormeille of the cathedral, Minor Canon de Lyra too, sometime Vicar of Diddlebury, Custos of the College of Vicars Choral for longer than any man since the reign of Elizabeth I, bassoon virtuoso, principal vocalist with choral societies throughout the kingdom and composer of the Christmas carol *Shine calm and bright* – as he described himself.[83] When questioned on the incidents Mr Duncombe said he couldn't imagine why an unfavourable comment as to technical matters should be objected to. The complainants were silly and absurdly touchy.[84] There are no recorded views of the ladies of the Herefordshire Philharmonic Society or of the Hereford Choral Society on The Revd W D V Duncombe, vicar choral at Hereford Cathedral, Minor Canon de Cormeille of the cathedral, Minor Canon de Lyra, Vicar of Diddlebury, Custos of the College of Vicars Choral for longer than any man since the reign of Elizabeth I. But Mr Sinclair was certainly never cowed by Mr Duncombe. At Sinclair's third Annual Meeting of the Choral Society in February 1892 the Custos ventured his opinions on the conductor's choice of the previous year's music. Dr Parry's *Ode to St Cecilia's Day* was of more appeal to music students than the general public, without one iota of dramatic interest. He knew two professional sopranos who took one look at the solo part and declined to have anything to do with it. And Mr Sinclair stood up and said how much he disagreed with Mr Duncombe.[85] Mr Duncombe evidently continued to offer gratuitous advice to the conductor. In 1908 he thought that the rehearsals on Walford Davies's *Everyman* were about as enjoyable as a military campaign.[86]

Meeting and quoted the words of the conductor: he and all the Society's officials desired, he said, 'to educate as many as possible, people of all grades of society, and associated with all religious sects and walks of life',[88] which received a ringing endorsement. This is the kind of Choral Society it was to remain throughout the twentieth century, a chorus of all sorts and conditions of men and women, or at least of a wide social background, of different denominations and of none, though it's true that Anglican clergymen have always been found strewn among the ranks as if by divine or at least diocesan ordinance.

Changing repertory and changing sensibilities

As the Choral Society became larger the repertory changed. Those concerts in the first twenty-five years – of men's and boys' voices – were essentially of two kinds. The first was of selections from big works. There might be numbers from *Messiah* in the first part, beginning with 'Behold the Lamb of God', and of *Judas Maccabaeus* in the second. Some of the concerts were sequences of choruses with arias or quartets interwoven, movements from *The Creation*, or from *The Seasons*, or from Beethoven's *The Mount of Olives*. There might be the *Dettingen Te Deum* in the first part, with the overture to *Berenice* opening the concert, and in the second the overture to Handel's *Alcina*, movements from Crotch's *Palestine* and an anthem like Croft's *God is gone up*.

The second kind of evening would consist of miscellaneous items in sequence: a movement from a Classical symphony, part-songs, songs, a glee, a madrigal, a piece for solo cornet, a nautical ballad, a hunting song. An operatic overture by Mozart might find itself next to Gibbons's *The silver swan*, or a symphony by Mozart next to a glee by Reginald Spofforth.

It may look like a hastily-prepared school concert of yesteryear, but it wasn't quite that. Grand 'Miscellaneous Concerts' were presented everywhere, all over Europe. Concerts like these miscellanies in Hereford were presented in Vienna, in Paris, in Oxford – as well as in London. And, as happened everywhere else, such ragbags at Hereford petered out at the beginning of the twentieth century.

In 1890 George Bernard Shaw thought that there were 'few things more terrible to a seasoned musician than a miscellaneous concert … A ballad concert, a symphony concert, a pianoforte recital: all these are welcome when they are not too long: but the old-fashioned "grand concert", with an overture here, a *scena* there, and a ballad or an instrumental solo in between, is insufferable.'[89] But such a concert plan was the creature of a different setting and different artistic norms. If there were a very limited number of concerts in a local-

There's no evidence that Dr Sinclair – as he had now become – took too much notice of Mr Duncombe's opinions.

The original members of the Choral Society were men and boys from poor families, and if not quite all the singers had cathedral connections or were members of Anglican congregations, it must have felt essentially an Anglican institution. Yet from its very earliest years it evidently attempted to cross denominational boundaries. The Wesleyans held an annual 'Tea Meeting' at Christmas in the 1840s. After tea at the meeting in December 1844 there were addresses by the Wesleyan Ministers, the Baptist Minister, the Primitive Methodist Minister, and the Minister of Lady Huntingdon's Chapel. And then, to present pieces of sacred music, members of the Society joined the choir of the Wesleyan Chapel and sang 'in very superior style'. It all 'afforded high gratification to the numerous assemblage'.[87]

Seventy years later, a local paper reported the Society's Annual

ity – as there would have been in most European towns and cities a hundred years before the mid-nineteenth century – a number of musicians would inevitably have claim on the audience's attention. The concert was a social occasion, and it was bad manners of the trombonist to outstay his welcome. It was conceded too that individuals in the audience would have different tastes and partialities, and all must be addressed, or at least some attempt must be made to enchant everyone. Those were the kind of considerations that were at the forefront of programme-planners' minds.

Practicalities certainly sometimes intervened, and a programme presented might be the result of accidents: at one Christmas meeting one of the finest airs in Dr Crotch's *Palestine*, perhaps *the* finest in the opinion of many Crotch-lovers, had to be left out. And why was this? Because somebody had lost the copy, as the critic noted drily.[90] He pointed out on another occasion the programme 'had too much of solo and verse: out of twenty-five to thirty vocal pieces it presented only eight or nine choruses'. At some earlier meetings there'd been hardly anything but choruses, a fault to be avoided just as much. 'The great desideratum on such occasions is variety.'[91]

Occasionally there were very unfortunate lapses and the *Hereford Times* simply had to draw attention to what it clearly considered wretched dumbing-down: 'The vocal pieces did not range very high … The foolish production called *The bells of St Michael's Tower*, the opening strain of which is a plagiarism from *Merrily, merrily, shall we live now*, was much better sung than it deserved; and the same remark to Bishop's *I love the hills*, Lover's *Fairy Tempter*, and some other specimens of the namby-pamby school … The trashy school of the day was duly represented by polkas, quadrilles founded on that characteristic specimen of American taste, *Bobbing around*'.[92]

Fifty years later, when Bernard Shaw himself kept on fuming about Grand Miscellanies, the world itself had changed and such categories and such touchstones no longer applied. The greatest shift in human consciousness since the Renaissance, which we call Romanticism, had changed the substance of music, the ways in which music was written and the ways it was listened to. Music was no longer the 'accompaniment to sociability' it had been in the previous century.[93] It was no longer, at it had been for Charles Burney in the eighteenth century, 'an innocent luxury, unnecessary to our being, but a great gratification and improvement of the sense of hearing'.[94] It was no longer enough to be entertained. It was something much more tremendous. Listen to E T A Hoffman, Elgar told his audience at his inaugural lectures at Birmingham: 'We speak a loftier language than mere human speech … in the wondrous accents of Music'. In music we are wafted upward 'to the realms of light, where we learn the mystery of our existence'.[95]

That was the characteristic tone of nineteenth-century Romanticism. The crucial European figure was Beethoven in his garrett, the seer, the solitary genius, but in English circles – in Anglican circles – Wordsworth was also a crucial formative influence. As a programme note for a Three Choirs performance of Beethoven's Violin Concerto characteristically showed, the English cast of mind is able to reconcile Beethoven and Wordsworth. The solitary genius of Beethoven is only one aspect of the picture, the writer explains. If he'd had the good fortune to have been a citizen of Gloucester or Worcester or Hereford, the writer implies, Beethoven would in fact have fitted in very well. Too often he's presented to us as 'a lonely, grief-laden Titan, pouring out his sorrows in music profound, sombre and tragic'. Well, that was part of the story. But it is not a wholly complete picture. He didn't go round shaking his fist at fate all the time. And he never would have done that in Hereford or Gloucester. 'His misfortunes, truly great, were matched by a fortitude equally great, and despite his deafness and his loneliness he never ceased to enrich the world with music such as this Concerto, full of those qualities which Wordsworth so desired in his poetry –

Truth, beauty, grandeur, love and hope,
Blessed consolation in distress
And joy in widest commonalty spread.'[96]

The more substantial oratorios began to find a regular place in Choral Society concerts – works like Mendelssohn's *St Paul* and *Elijah*, Haydn's *The Creation* and *The Seasons* – and not extracts from these but the works complete, or almost complete. And also with Handel, *Jephthah*, *Judas Maccabeus* and *Messiah*, which would constitute the whole of an evening's concert. Handel, Haydn and Mendelssohn long continued to act as models for new works and later the harmonic and formal procedures of Wagner were adopted and adapted in contemporary compositions. There were numerous large-scale cantatas, Dvořák's *The Spectre's Bride*, J F Barnett's *The Ancient Mariner*, Frederic Cowen's *St John's Eve* and later Elgar's cantata *Caractacus* and *King Olaf* and Coleridge-Taylor's cantatas, *The Song of Hiawatha*. Walford Davies's oratorio *Everyman* was sung in 1908. The most famous English oratorio of them all, Elgar's *Gerontius*, was sung by some members of the Choral Society at the Three Choirs in 1902, the first performance of *Gerontius* conducted by the composer, though it was not to be given by the Society itself until 1937. Granville Bantock said that Elgar wept while he was conducting that performance and that everyone was deeply affected. 'A most wonderful day to have had in one's life', Lady Elgar wrote in her diary.[97]

When they were first played in Hereford, Mozart and Haydn's large-scale pieces sat uncomfortably in the Grand Miscellaneous Concerts. In the 1850s the *Hereford Times* critic considered a performance of Haydn's 'Symphony No 1' – perhaps the first of the Salomon Symphonies, No 93 in D – was 'too long for the occasion',[98] and a few years later a Mozart symphony caused raised eyebrows, 'it having occupied *twenty-five minutes in performance*'.[99] And there were no words! What was it all about? On and on. But now, as the nineteenth century drew to its close, everything was being listened to in a different way. The overture to *Messiah* began with a proper E minor chord, the home key, yes, you knew where you were. Serious, certainly, but most beautiful. And you sat up, leaning on the back of your seat. You look around. You might even catch someone's eye. You might even smile.

But *Gerontius*? It starts on an A, and then there's a G sharp, an A, a G natural. Where are we? This requires a different kind of listening. Many in the audience look down. Chins are supported with a hand. Some legs are crossed. But it's not lounging. It's *intensity*.

At the beginning of *The Creation* after the orchestral introduction the chorus sings:

And the spirit of God moved upon the face of the water;
And God said; Let there be light! And there was light!

Until the second 'light' the chorus is singing *pianissimo*. And then it's a sudden *fortissimo,* a great blaze of sound. When this was sung in Vienna in 1806, the audience broke out in thunderous applause. Well, it was a performance to mark Haydn's seventy-sixth birthday and a sparkling occasion. But later on in the century sensibilities had changed, sounds were listened to differently, grasped differently. They probably wouldn't have clapped like that even in Vienna at the end of the century. They certainly wouldn't have burst out like that in Hereford.[100]

And so the agreeable Miscellaneous Concerts became less agreeable, and audiences as well as singers wanted to lose themselves in the profundities, intricacies and difficulties of music which was considered great, not diverting but profound – and not only mighty works of nineteenth- and later twentieth-century heroes, but the masters of the past too. For another result of Romanticism was the creation of the classical canon. The formation of the Bach Choir in London itself testifies both to social and musical shifts. It was the idea of a young lawyer called Arthur Coleridge, who had discovered Bach as an undergraduate at Cambridge. He suggested a performance of the Mass in B minor to his friend Otto Goldschmidt – this would be the first ever performance in England. Goldschmidt

was German and educated at the Leipzig Conservatoire, where his teachers included Mendelssohn, and the musical gods he was taught to revere included Johann Sebastian Bach. The first members of the Bach Choir were drawn from the upper levels of Victorian society and its rehearsal times reflected the needs of its members, late afternoon being ideal, provided the rehearsal concluded early enough to allow members time enough to dress for dinner. The rehearsals would start in November when members had all arrived in London for the season.[101]

Certainly there was growing enthusiasm for music and for singing among all classes of society. Mr Townshend Smith himself, the second conductor of the Society, began teaching singing as soon as he arrived in the city at the beginning of 1843.[102] The *Hereford Journal* was most impressed with Townshend Smith's initiative, his plan for 'diffusing a taste for the exquisite art' being 'most admirable'.[103] In the 1850s Mr Burvill in Commercial Street, at that time a lay clerk in the cathedral choir, was offering 'to the Clergy, Gentry, and Public generally' both individual singing lessons and classes 'for the cultivation of vocal music'. And on Thursday mornings at a quarter past twelve in St Peter's school room, he offered – at 2s 6d a quarter – a special 'Class for Ladies'.[104] In the early 1860s, Miss Paine, 'professor of music (pupil of Signor Crivelli in London)', at No 5, Barton Villas, had the honour of announcing singing lessons for 'the Nobility, Clergy, Gentry and Inhabitants of Hereford and the vicinity'.[105] And at the same time, in King Street, Mr C J H Wilkes too was running a 'Select Singing Class for Ladies'.[106]

But even in the 1880s the editor of *The Musical Times* had to admit that the prejudice against musicians might be waning but it was not yet extinct, and the conviction that 'musicians are as a class wanting in the manlier qualities … They are so firmly persuaded that exclusive devotion to the study of music is inevitably attended by a weakening of moral and physical fibre that they avoid all personal contact or association with such persons' was still prevalent.[107] A musical critic of that time remembered attending a meeting to discuss the creation of the Royal College of Music, which opened in 1882. The meeting was chaired by the Prince of Wales, and very important persons indeed had been summoned to give their views on this vital subject. There was Mr Gladstone; the Archbishop of Canterbury; Sir Stafford Northcote, the Chancellor of the Exchequer; and the future Prime Minister, Lord Rosebery. Each important person was asked for his views, and each began by reminding everyone that, of course, he knew nothing at all about music. But by the end of Victoria's reign, the writer was sure, there was less need for musicians and amateurs of music to be so defensive. There were still 'gentlemen of the old school' who displayed a smug pride when they

confessed they were unable to tell the difference between 'Yankee Doodle' and 'God save The Queen'. But there was much less prejudice and philistinism than there had been fifty years before. He put this down to Victoria herself and her consort, Prince Albert, 'an ardent worshipper of the art and a composer of merit'. And he dedicated a book of essays on music in England to Her Majesty The Queen, 'Friend of Mendelssohn and The First Englishwoman to Recognize the Genius of Wagner'.[108]

These were the kind of shifts in attitudes and sensibilities that had led to more and more educated and enthusiastic men and women coming forward to sing in the Choral Society in Hereford in 1900 than there were forty years earlier.

The Herefordshire Philharmonic Society

The prejudices of the gentlemen in Hereford against music and musicians and singing may also have been eroded a little because of the enthusiasms of the squire at Hampton Court, of the Arkwright family: family motto *Multa tuli fecique* – 'I have endured and done many things'.

This was the unconventional Johnny Arkwright, who came into his inheritance in 1858 at the age of twenty-four. It made him the largest landowner in Herefordshire. His eighteenth-century forebears had made their fortune through patenting a mechanical method of spinning yarn, and then by creating what was in effect the modern factory system.[109] He rode enthusiastically to hounds, he shot, he liked fishing and playing cricket; he managed his estates like a military exercise, and became very knowledgeable about land drainage systems; he was an expert breeder of Herefordshire bulls; he designed and patented his design for those rectangular wooden trays for transporting fruit and vegetables we still use. And he was not only a tremendous music-lover but himself a violinist. He liked playing best either on his 1732 Stradivarius or on a del Gesù from about the same period that he seems to have bought for himself on his twenty-fifth birthday. Quite where and how his musical enthusiasms were set alight and nourished and cultivated is unclear. His education, at Eton and Christ Church, Oxford would not normally have done anything but dampen them. Wishing to make music on a larger scale than the concert parties and chamber music sessions in which he regularly took part, he established the Herefordshire Philharmonic Society in 1863 'to promote instrumental and vocal practice among amateur musicians in Herefordshire'. The intention was to give two or more concerts annually to which only members and their guests were admitted. They would also give special concerts, maybe with other organisations or for specific charitable purposes, and sometimes there would not be full orchestral and choral forces but chamber groups. There would be a vocal and an instrumental practice during the first week of each month.[110]

Within a few months there was a membership of 126 non-performers, ninety-two vocalists and twenty-six instrumentalists. By 1865 the total had risen to 315. Because of his social connections Arkwright was able to entice, persuade or bully the gentry of Herefordshire to become subscribers. The Bosanquets, the Hoskyns, the Stanhopes, and the Clowes of Burton Court joined the Philharmonic. Among other early subscribers were the Batemans of Shobdon, the Cotterells of Garmons, the Clives of Whitfield Court, the Bulmers of Aylestone Hill and the Cornewalls of Moccas. In time Miss de Winton of Gratonbury became a subscriber, as did the Heywoods of Ocle Court, the Peploes of Garnstone and the Rankins of Brygwyn. The Rogers of Stanage Park joined and the Baileys of Glanusk Park near Crickhowell, the Crofts of Lugwardine Court, the Dunnes of Bircher Hall, and the Baskervilles of Clyro Court near Hay-on-Wye. It was easier to think of who hadn't joined than who had. Because of his work on committees – he served as chairman of the executive committee for Hereford's Three Choirs Festival and on the council of the Royal Agricultural Society of England – his connections were wide. If he didn't know someone he could easily arrange an introduction. The Philharmonic Society appointed Henry Leslie as musical director, one of the most renowned choral conductors of the day, and Sir Frederick Gore Ouseley, the Precentor at Hereford and Professor of Music at Oxford, as president. Not many of the landed gentry could sing or play an instrument at all, let alone to the standard Johnny Arkwright required, but a few did, and there were the younger sons, the clergymen, for whom it was perfectly acceptable.[111]

The Philharmonic Society had a category of honorary members, friends, members of the same social set as the founders that it wished to have as permanent guests, as it were, men like the The Revd J C Hanbury, who taught classics at the Cathedral School and was an excellent pianist. Sir Frederick Ouseley was another honorary member – besides his position as president – which allowed him to play the piano from time to time. He occasionally appeared in the Shirehall in January with an improvised solo.

For additional expert players the Society created another category, associate members, professional musicians, 'the players' who would help 'the gentlemen': the trombonist Mr Bishop, who lived in St Owen's Street, and Mr Brooke, who played the clarionet, from Bristol. And there was that family from Worcester boosting the strings, three of them, the Elgar brothers and the son of William. Edward, yes, Edward Elgar. In fact Elgar – the young one, quite a useful violinist – was leader of the band from 1891 until 1895. When Henry Leslie wasn't there to conduct, the Honourable Seymour 'Sim' Egerton, who became the Fourth Earl of Wilton and was a friend of Sir Arthur Sullivan, would take the baton.

After four years the *Hereford Times* gave a short account of the success of the Herefordshire Philharmonic Society, this 'association of amateurs' who had been steadily and quietly working in the border county 'for the purpose of bringing together all the amateur talent that existed in that and the neighbouring counties'. In a very short time, according to the *Times*, the Society had enrolled 'everyone of distinction and position among its members'. There was by this time a band of nearly fifty – including professional assistants – and the chorus numbered a hundred. Such a Society 'ought to

John Hunt

exercise much influence for good'. The column lists the works that had so far been performed. To the performances the writer should not allude, he explains, these being amateur musicians. But he will make one exception and mention the performance of a difficult work very finely executed by both band and chorus, Beethoven's *Choral Fantasy*, 'the pianoforte part being played by a lady, the representative of one of the oldest and most distinguished families in Herefordshire'.[112] Among Johnny Arkwright's musical friends were members of an ensemble called The Wandering Minstrels. This was a large group of amateur musicians created in 1860 from the ranks of the aristocracy and the military. Initially this was for their own enjoyment, but they soon began giving concerts all over the country to raise money for charities. Johnny Arkwright often drew on their ranks for his Hereford concerts. Sometimes they would be advertised in their own name, as playing with the Philharmonic Society, there being so many of them. They created a new way of experiencing music, the 'smoking concert' it was called, a social gathering at which gentlemen, and sometimes ladies too, would dine, drink, listen to the music and – but not the ladies – would smoke.[113]

From the Minstrels were recruited on several occasions men like Captain Le Patourel, who played the flute, and Captain Xavier Orange, who gave brilliant solos on the concertina, and Colonel De Bathe – who was to become General Sir Henry de Bathe – who did sterling service on the bass drum.[114] Certainly there were a considerable number of local residents who sang with both the Herefordshire Philharmonic Society and the Hereford Choral Society. The records of the Choral Society during the three and a half decades of the Philharmonic's life are very meagre. But some details from the Philharmonic's records seem likely to reflect the concerns and problems and difficulties which were experienced by the other choir.

Johnny Arkwright clearly loved making music. Everything he did he did with tremendous zest. He could quickly be spotted in public because of the peels of laughter that invariably kept bursting out round him. Even so, and notwithstanding the comparatively modest amounts of time the Philharmonic Society demanded of its musicians, 'laxity of attendance' became a problem now and then.[115] Leslie insisted on his 'guest conductor' status; he did not wish to impose repertory, though he would advise on the degree of difficulty likely to prove insurmountable to these singers. At one point he told the committee that, in choosing repertory for the current singers, they should select works which never exceed a range for the sopranos of from middle C to the A an octave and a sixth above, for the first altos of from A below middle C to E, the top space of the treble clef, and second altos of from G below middle C to E flat at the top of the treble clef. All the sopranos must not just be able to reach an A; they must be able to sustain it comfortably.[116]

He could help identify problems, but the members of the committee were the ones to solve them because they knew the individuals concerned very well, as he didn't.[117] Characteristic difficulties arose because of a small number of singers whose voices wouldn't blend. One or two of the ladies took away all brightness in the sopranos. Presumably this was because of the 'thickness' of their voices, or bad tuning, or because of a prominent vibrato. No remedy was possible, Mr Leslie was sure. He told the committee that he broke up his old London choir because it could be improved only by turning out veterans whose sole fault lay in their loyalty to him.[118] Sometimes ignorance and insensitivity murdered a performance. Strict discipline over attendance must be observed and enforced, he advises. And he gives a recent example: the singing at rehearsal of the madrigal *Sweet honey-sucking bees* was such as to astonish and delight. At the public performance some brand new sopranos insisted on singing an F sharp where the notation indicated an F natural. You must decide, Leslie told the committee, whether you wish to dismiss a bad singer, or to attempt improvement by ordering another voice test.[119] If bad singing is the result of an inability to read well enough, the singer concerned could be placed on a reserved list and encouraged to request another voice test after receiving further tuition in reading. He recommended a rule requiring new singers to attend a year's rehearsals before being allowed to take part in a public concert. He suggested the committee always discuss useful comments of choir members on different repertories. Some, though, should be ignored: in the 1880s at least the 'usual complainers' were 'the music-hallers' who insisted that the choir was 'too classical'.[120]

In the Philharmonic's concerts the chorus contributed madrigals from the Elizabethan period by composers like Bennett, Morley and Wilbye, as well as modern ones by Robert Pearsall. There would be glees and part-songs. They sang several part-songs by their conductor Henry Leslie, and they sang *Queen and huntress, chaste and fair* by the conductor of the Choral Society, Langdon Colborne. They sang anthems like Mendelssohn's *Hear my prayer* and there were solo songs, Purcell's *Nymphs and shepherds* and Schubert's *Who is Sylvia?* And these vocal pieces were set alongside piano solos, violin and piano movements, piano trios, string quartets and overtures for the whole band by Nicolai or Mendelssohn or there were whole symphonies by Haydn or Mendelssohn. Sometimes they sang longer choral works, a selection from *Alexander's Feast*, Sterndale Bennett's *The Woman of Samaria*, Arthur Somervell's cantata *The Forsaken Merman*. In other works they were very similar to the Grand Miscellaneous Concerts of both the Hereford Philharmonic Society – the club established by the vicars choral – and the earlier concerts of the Choral Society. Johnny Arkwright's Society held to such programmes really until the end of its life – its last concert seems to have been in 1898 – which old-fashioned format may have been one of the reasons for their demise. For the Choral Society were becoming more challenging in repertory and were setting higher standards in choral accomplishment. They had a young ambitious conductor and were presenting substantial works like *Elijah* and Berlioz's *Faust* and exciting modern pieces like Arthur Goring Thomas's *The Swan and Skylark* and Charles Villiers Stanford's *The Revenge* and even repeat performances of the Grand Choral March from Richard Wagner's *Tannhäuser* which the conductor was determined Hereford should like eventually. Then there was the trilogy *The Song of Hiawatha*. The score of *Hiawatha's Wedding Feast* was completed in May 1898 and first heard in Hereford in 1900; *The Death of Minnehaha* and *Hiawatha's Departure* were both completed in 1899 and first heard in Hereford in 1901. He was certainly no slouch, that Mr Sinclair at the Choral Society.

The nineteenth-century conductors
John Hunt, George Townshend Smith, Langdon Colborne and
George Robertson Sinclair

Who were these early conductors? By the end of the nineteenth century cathedral organists had become altogether more formidable figures than they had been previously. Many of them now possessed an authority and a kind of mystique which had not perhaps enveloped their predecessors. This derived partly from the new importance of music within the cathedral, itself one aspect of the spiritual reformation that was transforming English church life and touching the whole of English society.

In the middle of the nineteenth century the cathedral organist was a lowly figure in the cathedral close and in the social life of the cathedral city, and often an embattled one among the cathedral musicians themselves. Consider Arthur Corfe, the teacher of the Choral Society's founder. He came from a famous family of church musicians associated with Salisbury Cathedral for 170 years and was himself in charge of the music there from 1804 until 1863.[121] One of Dr Corfe's sons was elected to a choristership at Magdalen College, Oxford in 1814. Unlike other choral foundations Magdalen attracted choristers from all over the country. It had a boarding school and the scholarship given to choristers was continued until they had graduated. This astonishing generosity resulted in choristers from privileged as well as very poor backgrounds; fathers of choristers might be baronets or college servants, clergymen or bakers. The college authorities designated the father's occupation in its records. A father was either *Clerk* – a clerk in holy orders, a clergyman – *Gent*, a gentleman, a professional man with a Master of Arts degree, or *Pleb*, a college or domestic servant, a blacksmith, a cabinet maker, a coach-maker, a plumber or glazier. Corfe's father, a cathedral organist? Clearly the right category was *Pleb*.[122] But very gradually cathedral organists became professional men with both musical and personal authority. There were certainly nineteenth-century cathedral organists who had university degrees. But until the middle of the nineteenth century a music degree at Oxford or Cambridge simply required the presentation of an exercise, a musical composition, without any residence requirements. In the 1850s both universities introduced an additional examination. When Langdon Colborne, the Choral Society's third conductor, took his Cambridge degree in 1864, he would have submitted his composition and then found a college to give him a bed on the eve of the written examination; otherwise there were no residence requirements. That music began to be regarded with much more seriousness at universities, in cathedral worship and in society generally, owed much to the work and

George Townshend Smith (1875)

influence of The Revd Sir Frederick Ouseley, Precentor of Hereford between 1855 and 1889. He founded St Michael's College, Tenbury, which was intended to provide a model for cathedral worship.

As an apologist for cathedral music he spoke with very great authority. Until John Stainer there was no-one from within the ranks of cathedral musicians who would be listened to with greater respect and attention. Ouseley was the son of the Ambassador Extraordinary and Minister Plenipotentiary to the Persian Court, the godson of the Duke of York and the Duke of Wellington, rich, privileged and convinced of the power of music and the necessity of it as a handmaid of religion.

He was a musical prodigy. When as an undergraduate he announce to the startled Dean of Christ Church that he was going to take a degree in music, he was told that it was 'utterly derogatory for a man in his social position to entertain such an idea'.[123] The high seriousness with which he invested his college at Tenbury would certainly have been felt by the third and fourth of the Society's conductors: Langdon Colborne, organist at St Michael's, and George Robertson Sinclair, a chorister there.[124] John Hunt (1806–42) was a chorister at Salisbury under Arthur Corfe and then articled to him, and was appointed organist at Hereford in 1835 when he was twenty-eight. 'His talents were at all times equally at the command of his friends, the public, or the distressed', it was said of him, and he seems to have won the hearts of the unconfident young men in the choral society and of the very confident vicars choral in the band.[125]

One evening in November 1842 Mr Hunt was leaving the Audit Dinner at the cathedral on his way to a concert in the Shirehall. He was 'proceeding with the quick and ready step with which he ever attended to his duties.' He seems to have stumbled on a tray which had been left carelessly on the ground in the dark of the College Cloisters, and in falling he smashed a tureen and cut his wrist badly on its broken edge. His wound became infected and in a week he lay dead. He was thirty-five. Three days after he died his fifteen-year-old nephew, a chorister who lived with him and his wife in Castle Street, died of a broken heart, they said. On the day of the funerals there were crowds about the close and in and about Castle Street. His widow and other relatives and members of the Choral Society were ranged on each side of the two biers as the funeral train left the house of the deceased and wended its way into the cathedral. Inside there was a majestic silence as the two coffins were taken into the Lady Chapel. There were crowds there too. Many were overcome by the intensity of it all and the sadness and the sorrow. Dean Merewether, who had insisted on taking the service himself, was frequently unable to proceed for tears. Even the officers of the cathedral, the vergers, inured to scenes of grief and mourning, were seen leaning against the pillars sobbing like children.[126]

John Hunt was succeeded in 1843 by George Townshend Smith (1813–77), who had come from St Margaret's, King's Lynn, chosen out of forty-two candidates. Townshend Smith was the son of a lay clerk at St George's Chapel, Windsor, where he himself had been a chorister, and he later studied with Samuel Wesley. Townshend Smith was appointed on the basis of outstanding testimonials, and he lived up to them in all respects, both as a musician and as a man. He seemed to win everyone over very quickly. He arrived in Hereford in January and had to handle a festival at once later that same year. Wisely perhaps he wasn't particularly adventurous this first time – there was Handel's *Dettingen Te Deum*, Tallis's 'sublime' responses, *Zadok the Priest*, *Messiah* and *The Creation* – and all this was sympathetically commented upon: Mr Townshend Smith had not 'pandered to a false and depraved *fashion*, but has chosen rather to fall back upon good, sound, sterling, classical music'.[127] His play-

Langdon Colborne

ing of the piano and organ was much admired, as were his songs and also his singing. He took part in the annual concert of the Cathedral School at Christmas in 1867 and, as he always did, sang 'faultlessly'.[128] There are glimpses of the admiration and love that his pupils and friends felt for him: on Christmas Day 1860 the choristers presented him with a very beautiful envelope case, inkstand, and writing book 'as a token of regard to their respected organist'.[129] In 1846 a London singer called John Parry wrote to him after the Three Choirs Festival, congratulating him on behalf of all the visiting musicians for his abilities as a conductor and thanking him for his kindness towards them on all occasions.[130] In 1858 the visiting orchestral musicians wrote a similar letter after their visit expressing their gratitude for his 'kind, considerate, and gentlemanly treatment' of them and sending best wishes to him and his family.[131] The local critics always praised him and acknowledged his authority: 'that very respectable and estimable gentleman … the admitted Co-

HEREFORD CHORAL SOCIETY
(Established 1839).

GRAND ✦ CONCERT

IN THE

Shire-Hall, Tuesday, Nov. 28th, 1899.

PRINCIPALS:

MISS EDITH KINGSFORD.   MR. LANE WILSON

Solo Violin: Solo Harp:

MR. DONALD HEINS.   MISS MIRIAM TIMOTHY

Accompanist: MR. P. C. HULL

FULL BAND AND CHORUS OF 200 PERFORMERS.

Conductor: **DR. G. R. SINCLAIR**

✦ PROGRAMME ✦

PART I.

1. OVERTURE   ...   .   "Alphonso and Estrella." Op. 69   ...   ...   Schubert
2. **"HERO AND LEANDER,"**
    A Dramatic Cantata by C. H. Lloyd.
3. SONG   ...   .   "Far Greater in his Lowly State"   ...   ...   Gounod
    MISS EDITH KINGSFORD.
4. PRELUDE AND RONDO for Violin and Orchestra   ...   ...   Donald Heins
    MR. DONALD HEINS.
5. GIPSY SONGS   ...   { (a) "Sound the Pipe and Tabor" }   ...   Bendl
                     { (b) "Songs my Mother taught me" }
    MR. LANE WILSON.

During the interval Doctor of Music's Robes will be presented to Dr. Sinclair by the Lord Bishop.

PART II.

6. **"THE REVENGE,"**
    A Ballad of the Fleet, for Chorus and Orchestra, by C. Villiers Stanford.
7. SONG   ...   .   "My Dearest Heart"   ...   ...   Sullivan
    MISS EDITH KINGSFORD.
8. HARP SOLOS ...   { (a) "Watching the Wheat" }   ...   J. Thomas
                       { (b) "Spring" }
    MISS MIRIAM TIMOTHY.
9. OLD ENGLISH SONG   ...   "The Pretty Creature" ...   ...   Arranged by Lane Wilson
    MR. LANE WILSON.
10. PATRIOTIC SONG   ...   ...   "Rule Britannia"   ...   ...
    The National Anthem.

Doors open at 7-30 p.m.   To commence at 8.   Carriages, 10-15.

Tickets—First Division, 4/- (3 for 10/6); Second Division, 2/-; Third Division, 1/-;

To be obtained of Messrs. Heins & Co., Broad Street; Messrs. Jakeman & Carver, High Town; Messrs. Wilson & Phillips,
Eign Street; and Mr. W. Mason, High Town.

WILSON & PHILLIPS, HEREFORD.

ryphaeus of matters musical amongst us'. And if there were defects at a concert they were swift to exculpate him: 'of course we impute no official dereliction to our popular organist'.[132] If anyone was to get the Choral Society out of a jam it was Mr Townshend Smith, who, no doubt on more than one occasion, 'earned the gratitude of his choir by the kindly tact with which he occasionally gave a little timely assistance when required'.[133]

What were rehearsals like? How did he teach the Choral Society a new work? It's almost impossible to say. His submissions to the Dean and Chapter on the choir were always intelligent, practical and lucid. He understood the difficulties faced by lay clerks: 'Hurried from secular employment at the Call of the Bell – a Surplice thrown over Mechanics Clothes – anxious to get through the Choral Service because it interferes with their other labours, frequently soliciting leave of absence suffering from illness caused by

incessant occupation … I am fully aware of the present evils and shall be delighted at their Removal.'[134] He himself managed to remain on friendly terms with the Chapter, the lay clerks and even the vicars choral, with individuals or factions that were hardly able to tolerate each other's presence. Speaking to the Chapter he was always respectful and discreet without fawning. He mentioned to the Chapter that some of them had often said he should be better paid. He left that in their hands, confident that they would give the matter proper consideration. And he thanked them for the extreme kindness they had always shown him, sustaining him through the 'dispiriting cathedral duty' that has devolved on him and keeping alive his hopes and determination for future improvement in the services that he so loved.[135] He died suddenly, aged only sixty-four, and his death came just before the start of a Choral Society rehearsal; everyone went home tearful and ashen-faced. The death of his beloved daughter the year before, aged only twenty-eight, he seemed to have borne with wonderful fortitude. But perhaps he had never quite recovered from the shock.

On the Sunday after he died the organ was left unplayed in tribute. On the day of his funeral the principal shops in Hereford were closed and the blinds of many private houses were drawn down.[136] The cathedral was full long before the service began. People noticed how wide a section of society was represented at his funeral: the poor, the rich, tradesmen, professional people, musicians, the county gentry, and all remembered an excellent intelligent musician and a courteous, kindly, amiable Christian gentlemen.

He was succeeded in 1877 by a much more shadowy figure, Langdon Colborne (1835–89), a pupil of John Stainer's organ teacher, George Cooper, organist at the Chapel Royal, who would become Stainer's assistant at St Paul's. Before he came to Hereford he was for fourteen years organist at St Michael's, Tenbury and then briefly at Beverley Minster, and the parish churches at Wigan and Dorking.

He introduced Parts I and II of Bach's *Christmas Oratorio* at the Three Choirs Festival in 1879 and the *Magnificat* in 1882, half a century before Bach was sung by the Choral Society alone. Langdon Colborne was unfortunate though in his choice of 'novelties', of the new works he commissioned for the festivals. There was the oratorio for Hereford that Dr Smith from Dublin composed about a godly youth called Kevin who wishes to devote his life to the service of heaven. But Kathleen has other ideas. And in the end she stands on a rock and laughs at him. He does manage to save himself from her clutches but only by hurling her shrieking into the black lake. Whether it was the text – 'more than usually unpoetical' was the opinion of one critic[137] – or the music itself – the accompaniments were rather elaborate and the orchestration rather heavy in parts,

George Robertson Sinclair

another commentator thought[138] – is not now quite clear. At any rate *Saint Kevin* was not adjudged a success by competent critics. Neither was another Colborne commission. Dr Garrett wrote *The Shunamite* for Hereford, and this too was remembered by almost no-one with much enthusiasm. The newspaper reviews elucidated fully the action of the oratorio and gave the names of the soloists but didn't convey much impression of the music, which impres-

sion 'was not so favourable as might have been anticipated from the name and position of the composer' in the words of the man from *The Manchester Weekly Times*.[139] The fact that Dr Garrett came from St John's College, Cambridge though, another hinted, might have been at the root of the problem. He could find little more to say than that *The Shunamite* was 'a carefully-compiled piece' which 'shows very scholastic treatment'.[140]

HEREFORD CHORAL SOCIETY
(Established 1839)

GRAND CONCERT

IN THE
SHIREHALL, TUESDAY, NOV. 27TH, 1900.

PRINCIPALS.

**Miss Gleeson-White   Miss Marian Blinkhorn
Mr. Montague Borwell**

Solo Violin: Solo Violoncello:
Mr. Donald Heins   Miss May Mukle

Accompanist: MR. P. C. HULL, L.R.A.M.

Conductor   -   -   **Dr. SINCLAIR**

PROGRAMME.

PART I.

1. MADRIGAL ... ... "Thyrsis, sleepest thou?" ... ... *Bennet*
2. SONGS ... ... { (a) "Le Baiser" ... ... *Goring Thomas*
                       { (b) "Viens, Aurore" (Old French) ... *Arranged by A.I.*
   MISS GLEESON-WHITE.
3. VIOLONCELLO SOLO ... ... "Variations sur un thème rococo" ... ... *Tschaikowsky*
   MISS MAY MUKLE.
4. SONG ... ... "The Yeoman's Wedding" ... ... *Poniatowski*
   MR. MONTAGUE BORWELL.
5. PART SONG ... ... "Purple glow the forest mountains" ... ... *Pearsall*
6. SONG ... ... "Mon cœur s'ouvre à ta voix" ... ... *Saint Saens*
   MISS MARIAN BLINKHORN.
7. PART SONG (for Female Voices, with accompaniment for two Violins and Pianoforte) "Fly singing bird" *Elgar*

PART II.

1. TRIO for Pianoforte, Violin, and Violoncello, in F. Op. 72. ... ... *Godard*
   Allegro Moderato.   Adagio.   Vivace.   Allegro Vivace.
   DR. SINCLAIR, MR. DONALD HEINS, AND MISS MAY MUKLE.
2. SONG ... ... "Endymion" ... ... *Liza Lehmann*
   MISS GLEESON-WHITE.
3. CHORUS ... ... "Now sets the sun" (St. Christopher) ... ... *Horatio Parker*
4. TRIO ... ... "Queen of the Night" ... ... *Smart*
   MISS GLEESON-WHITE, MISS MARIAN BLINKHORN, AND MR. MONTAGUE BORWELL.
5. SONG ... ... "Young Dietrich" ... ...*Henschel*
   MR. MONTAGUE BORWELL.
6. VIOLONCELLO SOLOS ... ... { (a) "Moment Musical" ... ... *Schubert*
                              { (b) "Scherzo" ... ... *Herbert*
   MISS MAY MUKLE.
7. SONG ... ... "Love the Pedlar" ... ... *E. German*
   MISS MARIAN BLINKHORN.
8. PART SONG (accompanied) ... ... "Vineta" ... ... *Brahms*
   The National Anthem.

Doors open at 7·30 p.m.   To commence at 8.   Carriages, 10·15
Tickets—First Division, 4/- (3 for 10/6); Second Division, 2/6; Third Division, 1/-;
To be obtained of Messrs. Heins & Co., Broad Street; Messrs. Jakeman & Carver, High Town; Messrs. Wilson & Phillips, High Street; and Mr. W. Mason, High Town.

WILSON & PHILLIPS, HEREFORD.

Langdon Colborne 'did all that within him lay' as a conductor, the *Gloucester Citizen* told its readers, but he was not really one of those 'who were born to wield the baton'.[141] His conducting 'lacked grip and spirit', they said.[142] *The Musical Times* felt that it should remind its readers that Dr Colborne was, after all, called away from the organist's bench to be a conductor only once in three years.[143] His last months make sad and melancholy reading. At his last Hereford festival, in his performance of selections from Handel's *Samson*, 'all was confusion, even the Conductor seeming not to know, at times, what should come next'. He directed at that festival a performance of his own cantata *Samuel*. It was intended to be within the capabilities of parish church choirs and was 'manifestly out of place' in the cathedral executed by a large choir, with organ and string band accompaniment.[144] To its readers the *Birmingham Daily Post* explained that the cantata took the place of the anthem, and so, as its

performance 'was a devotional exercise, criticism would be a breach of good taste'.[145] He died from the effects of diabetes on the day after his fifty-fourth birthday and only six months after his marriage to a lady from Tenbury.[146]

There then arrived in Hereford George Robertson Sinclair, much better remembered, even if his bulldog Dan is more often recalled than he himself. Perhaps bearing in mind Dr Colborne's limitations as an orchestral conductor the Chapter made quite clear in the job description that his successor should possess the skills of organist, choirmaster, and choral and orchestral conductor.[147] At Hereford the position of the organist was still particularly difficult when Sinclair arrived because, though he directed the services, the Precentor had theoretical responsibility for the music in the cathedral, the Succentor practical responsibility, and the vicars choral considered they were the experts in all matters musical and had ultimate authority. This situation could even result in public disputes about the speed at which an anthem should be sung. Sinclair demonstrated that he was in charge simply by taking charge, even when he wasn't, as in 1894, when it was pointed out that he was responsible for the choristers' behaviour only when they were outside the cathedral, not when they were in the choirstalls, when the Succentor (wielding the delegated authority of the Precentor) was actually in charge of them.[148] Sinclair didn't contest such pettifogging anachronisms; he simply ignored them. In 1907, on the death of the postholder, Sinclair was appointed additionally Succentor by the Chapter, which post had hitherto always been held by a member of the College of Vicars Choral, who duly pronounced it an outrage.[149] Why was Sinclair able to assume a commanding role in the direction of the music and the leadership of the men and boys and in conducting the choral society? How did he earn the respect of the Chapter and the respect and perhaps the fear at least of some in the Choral Society? Why did he inspire awe?

George Robertson Sinclair was the son of a colonial administrator in India. He was educated at St Michael's, Tenbury as a chorister and seemed destined for ordination. But he studied at the Royal Irish Academy of Music in Dublin under the organist of Christ Church Cathedral there, the formidable and distinguished Robert Prescott Stewart, and then served as an apprentice to C H Lloyd at Gloucester Cathedral. At the astonishingly young age of seventeen he was appointed organist at Truro Cathedral, where he worked closely with the Bishop, Edward Benson, the future Archbishop of Canterbury. As no Dean had yet been appointed, Benson acted as both Dean and Bishop. The Bishop told his organist that while he had musical expertise and the energy of a boy, 'you must do what you're told.' Sinclair was constantly consulting the Bishop, seek-

Dan, Sinclair's brindle bulldog, used to attend every Choral Society rehearsal. This pencil drawing, 'The Metamorphosis of Dan', was made by a member of the Society *during a rehearsal*. The name of the sinner is not recorded.

was constantly lit up too by rippling laughter. It's not surprising that he attracted over 400 working-class men and boys to the night schools he started in Lincoln. Nor is it surprising that the young organist developed under his guidance certain qualities of decisive leadership and empathetic understanding.[151] Sinclair's will to succeed was undoubtedly bolstered by his contact with such a man. He was responsible for the complicated musical arrangements of the consecration service at which many representatives of cathedral choirs were present, and he directed a series of diocesan choral festivals which brought together about 4000 singers from all over the diocese.[152] These early opportunities no doubt helped develop in him an assurance and authority in dealing with both musicians and with cathedral dignitaries. He became organist for the Grand Lodge of England and Supreme Grand Chapter of the Royal Arch of Freemasons.

He expected the choristers to behave, and they were coming now from homes which inculcated a certain respect for parents and other figures of authority. Sinclair was indeed a very competent conductor, and besides the Hereford Choral Society, he directed the Herefordshire Orchestral Society, the Crickhowell Musical Society, Ross Musical Society, and Herefordshire Choral Union. In July 1900 he was chosen unanimously – first by the committee and afterwards by the members – as the conductor of the Birmingham Festival Choral Society, one of the leading choral societies in England. Fifty years earlier, an American choir-trainer went round Europe listening to choirs. He thought that the world could never have heard a better performance than the Birmingham Chorus's of Handel's *Samson*, and he was convinced that 'in no place on earth can such a band and chorus be brought together, except in Birmingham'. Sinclair's selection by Birmingham was a great tribute to his musical skills and his personal qualities.

Sinclair was bold and adventurous in seeking out and then programming new music. In his first Three Choirs Festival at Hereford he included Wagner's Prelude to *Parsifal*, the first occasion on which it would heard in an English cathedral, which programming greatly impressed Elgar. He was tall, slim, and an excellent organist, whose virtuoso pedalling technique – *The Musical Times* referred to his 'pedalosity' – may have been inspired by his teacher in Dublin, Sir Robert Stewart, who had discovered a new kind of pedal virtuosity among organists in Paris in the 1850s. In January 1904, at the presentation of the annual report for 1903, Sinclair explained how he would like to encourage singers in other choirs in Hereford to use the Choral Society to their mutual benefit. They could help the Choral Society by joining; in the Society they might sing different kinds of music to those they sang habitually in their own choirs.

ing his instructions and advice. It was like being a school prefect, Sinclair said later, with the Bishop as headmaster.[150] And this was no ordinary headmaster, no ordinary Bishop. Benson had already created Wellington College in Berkshire, and had been a dynamic canon chancellor at Lincoln, where he had established the theological college. He'd turned down a professorship at Cambridge and the bishopric at Calcutta, all before he was appointed to Truro. After Truro he became Archbishop of Canterbury. He was a dignified presence, but full of nervous energy; he walked with quick, strong steps. His darting intellect played upon a most beautiful face, which

The music might be more difficult and challenging which could only help them, expand their horizons and develop their vocal skills. In the Choral Society they might find themselves next to a better singer, which would be another great advantage. He knew that practically all the singers in some of the city's choirs were already in the Choral Society. But there were some where this was not so, and he had been round talking to organists, choirmasters, and official members of the different choirs of the churches and chapels and hoped that this would encourage new members.[153]

There were other social factors that gave such a man as Sinclair greater authority in the community. The landowning families of Herefordshire faced growing economic calamities during the later 1870s and '80s. They were facing the prospect of disturbing falls in the value of their assets, partly through the increased importation of cheap meat; their wings were being clipped. The Hereford festival of 1882 was disastrous financially. The losses were much greater than anyone could reasonably have expected and of the Stewards, still at that time county grandees, half refused to pay the share they had guaranteed. They had hitherto been the festival authorities, taking decisions not only on festival administration and organisation, but on musical questions as well, however meagre their qualifications. With their failure to give reliable financial guarantees, their control over other aspects of the festival began to decline and the new, energetic, better educated organists and choirmasters stepped in with newfound assurance.[154]

A Festival Choral Society

It was only now, at the turn of the century, that the Festival Chorus was made up entirely of local singers, first in 1892 at the Gloucester festival, then at Hereford in 1897 and then at Worcester in 1902.[155] At earlier festivals the singers came from London – from St Paul's, Westminster Abbey, the Chapel Royal and the King's Concert – and from the chapels of Oxford and Cambridge. There were visitors too in different years from the choral societies in Lichfield, Birmingham, Cardiff and Liverpool, and especially from the north of England, from Yorkshire and Lancashire. The precise constitution of the Festival Chorus changed each year. This wasn't only because the three counties were much less densely populated than the industrial north, it was also that the tradition of choral singing was much stronger in certain regions of England than in others. It was the Evangelical Movement in the eighteenth century that had given rise to the popularity of the hymn. It was the Oxford Movement in the nineteenth that led to the general acceptance of hymn-singing in the Anglican Church; *Hymns Ancient and Modern* was first published in 1861. But the regular singing of hymns and the love of hymn-singing didn't happen overnight. Many cathedral musicians were lukewarm in their response to hymn-singing since hymns were essentially for congregations and not for their highly-trained choirs.

Working-class non-conformists, both Baptists and Methodists, cultivated congregational singing, usually unaccompanied congregational singing, and singing was a way of life. Before hymn-singing became an integral part of their worship, Anglicans found reason to fault it and to condemn singing. East Anglia was a Methodist stronghold, and in 1805 a clergyman in Ipswich pointed to a particular iniquity of Methodism, as he saw it. The labourer went home at the end of the day utterly exhausted, but instead of taking his rest, he immediately took his wife and children from the spinning wheel or other useful employment and, wasting money through the necessity of keeping the fire alight and burning candles, they would begin singing hymns. 'I have often heard this singing in some of our poorest cottages at so late an hour as nine, and sometimes later of a winter's evening.'[156] Already in the middle of the eighteenth century Anglicans feared the expertise that was developing in Methodist churches and the popularity of the music. The Archbishop of Canterbury was warned in the 1760s that 'the Sectarists gain a multitude of followers by their better singing.' And in 1769 the Chaplain-in-Ordinary to George III, in a reference to the singing of Methodists, urged that 'it is lawful to learn even from an enemy'.[157]

Many non-conformists took part in the Handel celebrations in 1784, and they were targeted particularly by the social reformers of the industrial revolution through the singing classes that were springing up everywhere encouraging 'rational amusement'. These were the endeavours of men like the Yorkshire Congregationalist John Curwen with his tonic sol-fa method and John Hullah, a Worcester man who in 1872 was appointed the government inspector of music in teacher training colleges all over the country. The real strength of the traditions lay with the working-class and with non-conformity. John Hullah himself noticed that among 'the higher and middle classes' gentlemen were 'much more ready to encourage their workmen or servants to sing, than their sons and daughters'.[158] Gentlemen would be likely to be condescending about singing classes and repeat the hoary old chestnut of Mr Hullah creating a hullaballoo all over the place.[159]

But there were many more gentlemen who were also talented singers in Hereford in 1900 than there were half a century earlier. Of course the city was twice as big now as when the Choral Society was established.[160] It might be true, Elgar said in his Birmingham lectures, that they no longer had those superb solo voices of a bygone age. What they did have now in the 1900s, he was sure, was a

Postcard from the 1920s

whole host of choral singers, 'a more earnest band of workers, educated men and women moreover, than ever before existed'.[161]

In 1899, when Sinclair was given a Lambeth doctorate, his friends in the choral societies he conducted subscribed to the purchase of his doctoral robes. In the interval of the Choral Society's concert in 1899 there was a little ceremony performed by the Dean as President of the Society. He proposed a vote of congratulation, which was seconded by Sir James Rankin, MP for Hereford, and then the Bishop presented Dr Sinclair with an album containing the names of the subscribers. He retired for a few moments and then reappeared – to an outburst of applause – in his yellow and scarlet robes. He had

been very proud a few days earlier, he said, when he had heard that, on the advice of a few of the most eminent musicians of the day, the Archbishop intended to confer on him a Lambeth doctorate. He was even more proud, he said, to stand there before his singers and to receive this tribute from all his friends in his choral societies.[162]

Even the *Gloucester Citizen* had to concede that in *Acis and Galatea* in November 1901 the Hereford band and chorus 'were never heard to better advantage'.[163] And in November 1902, when Elgar's *Coronation Ode* was given in Hereford, even the *Worcestershire Chronicle* had to admit that the Choral Society had given 'a capital performance'.[164]

The Twentieth-Century Choral Society

The twentieth-century choir: size and repertory

In 1855 there had been twenty-three voices singing, eight trebles and fifteen men. One singer remembered that there were six lay clerks and nine other men.[1] In the first year with ladies singing, in 1863, there were seventy adult voices, twenty-one women and forty-nine men, together with ten or twelve choristers.[2] In the concert in April 1891 there were 110 men's and women's voices and the choristers; in the November concert that year eighty-eight voices with the additional choristers. During the twentieth century there were typically between 150 and 200. In 1900 it was thought that there were on the register the highest number anybody could remember, 155 members; by 1908 though the number had risen to 172 in the Spring term, and in the autumn to 214, with 102 sopranos, fifty altos, twenty-two tenors and forty basses with an average attendance at rehearsals being 164. On the eve of the Great War, in 1913, there were 195 performing members, ninety-two sopranos, forty-nine altos, twenty tenors and thirty-four basses. During the war numbers did dip. But in the Spring of 1915 there were still 122 on the books and in the autumn of that year 161. In October 1919 there were 'about 170' on the register.[3] Between the wars there were generally slightly fewer singers than just before the First War; in 1923 there were 160 members with an average attendance of 125 and a best attendance at a rehearsal of 136.[4]

For *Gerontius* in 1989 there were 184 singers, eighty sopranos, seventy-one altos, sixteen tenors and thirty-seven basses. For the Monteverdi *Vespers* in 1999 there were sixty sopranos, sixty-seven altos, sixteen tenors and thirty-three basses, 176 singers in all. For *Gerontius* in 2004 there were 162 singers, fifty-five sopranos, sixty-seven altos, twelve tenors and twenty-eight basses.[5] For the Verdi *Requiem* in March 2012 there were fifty-five sopranos, sixty-two altos, fourteen tenors and thirty-one tenors, 162 voices in all.[6]

The Choral Society have usually sung sacred works in their concerts in the twentieth century. In the last four decades – when concerts were always given in the cathedral – the only works sung that could really be considered secular were Elgar's *Music Makers*, Coleridge-Taylor's *Hiawatha's Wedding Feast* and Lambert's *Rio Grande*. In earlier decades though when concerts were usually given in the Shirehall secular works presented included Gounod's *Faust*, Elgar's *Black Knight*, *Caractacus* and *In the Bavarian Highlands* – these four in the first decade of the century – and Edward German's *Merrie England*, which was given on three occasions by Percy Hull, in 1922, 1944, and 1949. Dvořák's *Spectre's Bride* was given in 1924 and Bizet's *Carmen* was given concert performances in 1931 and 1940 and 1962. Purcell's *Dido and Aeneas* was given in 1953 and in 1958 and George Dyson's *The Canterbury Pilgrims* in 1958 and his *In honour of the City of London* in 1933 and Vaughan Williams's *Five Tudor Portraits* in 1967. Most of these earlier concerts were given in the Shirehall. The Choral Society presented Smetana's *The Bartered Bride* in an arrangement by Julius Harrison at the Hillside Ballroom – also known as the Redhill Hostel – in 1956, nine years that is before the Rolling Stones appeared at the same venue.[7]

Concerts have often been devoted to a single work, *Elijah*, the Mass in B minor, Beethoven's *Missa Solemnis*, Rossini's *Petite Messe Solennelle*, Verdi's *Requiem*. Sometimes two choral works, like Fauré's *Requiem* and Britten's *St Nicolas*, have been sung together or sometimes two and an orchestral piece, with Schubert's 'Unfinished' Symphony in between Dvořák's *Te Deum* and Howard Ferguson's *The Dream of the Rood*, for example. The first performance of a major work of Bach was in 1930 when a selection of movements from Bach's Mass in B minor were sung; the work was given complete in 1933 and 1936 and 1945. The *St John Passion* was not done until 1953, the *St Matthew* Passion not until the following year. The only seventeenth-century music sung apart from Purcell's *Dido and Aeneas* was his *Ode for St Cecilia's Day* in 1968 and the Monteverdi *Vespers* which have been sung three times, in 1977, 1986 and 1999.

Six of the works which were sung between 1900 and 1914 found a place in the Society's programmes in the first decade of the twenty-first century: these were Mendelssohn's *St Paul*, Haydn's *The Creation*, Coleridge-Taylor's *Hiawatha's Wedding Feast*, and Handel's *Messiah* and *Judas Maccabaeus*. Parry was represented in both periods even if the same works weren't heard. Mozart's Mass in

C minor was sung in 2000 and the *Coronation Mass* in 2003 but neither were sung in those years at the beginning of the twentieth century. Neither was Mozart's *Requiem* which was sung in 2006 though this was performed in 1915. Brahms's *Requiem* which was sung in 2003 appears not to have been performed until 1948 when the new edition of Ivor Atkins, the organist at Worcester, was used. The only Brahms before that seems to have been the *Alto Rhapsody*, performed in 1946. The Choral Society sang Fauré's *Requiem* and Duruflé's *Requiem* in the first years of the twenty-first century but no French works a century before though they did do Berlioz's *Faust* in 1899. Very little French music has ever been sung; Fauré's *Requiem* seems to have sung for the first time in 1946. There was no Bach in the 1900s whereas in the 2000s there were the *St Matthew Passion*, the Mass in B minor, the *Magnificat* and Cantata *Nun ist das Heil und die Kraft* BWV 50. In the 1900s six works by Elgar were performed – this was the period in which he lived in Hereford – but not *Gerontius* nor *The Kingdom*, which last wasn't performed at all by the Society until 2006. The music sung in the 2000s but not yet composed in 1914 included Constant Lambert's *The Rio Grande* (completed 1927), Walton's *Belshazzar's Feast* (1931), Tippett's *A Child of Our Time* (1941), the Duruflé *Requiem* (1947), Finzi's *Intimations of Immortality* (1950), Poulenc's *Gloria* (1960), and William Mathias's *This Worlde's Joie* Op. 67 (1974).

Several of the works sung a hundred years ago are today almost totally forgotten. Sinclair himself must have rated Arthur Goring Thomas's *Swan and Skylark* highly: he programmed it in 1896 and 1902, and again in 1914. Long forgotten by almost everyone today is Frederic Cowen's *St John's Eve*, though having sung it 1912 the Society sang it again in 1920. And Coleridge-Taylor's *Tale of Old Japan* was sung in 1914, 1926 and 1932, the last a broadcast performance. The best-known of these forgotten works was Sullivan's *The Golden Legend* which demonstrated, according to one commentator, that even if the composer wrote no other work that will last, this one at least would 'hand the composer's name down to posterity'.[8]

Since 1900 the most frequently performed work has been *Messiah*. It was sung annually in whole or in part at the Three Choirs from at least 1876 until 1963, except for 1955.[9] Between 1900 and 1979 the Choral Society sang it sixteen times. It was not sung at all between 1905 and 1918, nor between 1924 and 1939. But since 1980 it has been sung annually.

There has been comparatively little contemporary music in the Society's own concerts: Melville Cook programmed Geoffrey Bush's cantata *In Praise of Mary* in 1958 and again in 1965; it had first been performed at the 1955 Three Choirs Festival. In 1959 he did John Gardner's *Seven Songs* Op. 36 for chorus and small orchestra, writ-

WORD BOOK—ONE SHILLING.

CENTENARY CELEBRATION
OF
Hereford Choral Society
(1837—1937)
II

A Special Performance of

**"THE DREAM
OF
GERONTIUS"**

IN *Elgar*
HEREFORD CATHEDRAL
ON
Thursday, 25th November, 1937
at 7-20 p.m.

SOLOISTS :

Astra Desmond   **Heddle Nash**

Arthur Cranmer

The City of Birmingham Orchestra
(Principal 1st Violin : ALFRED CAVE)

Organists :
Sir IVOR ATKINS, D.Mus., and Mr. HERBERT SUMSION, B.Mus.

FULL ORCHESTRA AND CHORUS OF 300

Conductor   :   Dr. PERCY C. HULL

A collection will be taken at the doors, as at the Three Choirs Festivals, for the benefit of the widows and orphans of clergy of the dioceses of Gloucester, Hereford and Worcester.

THE HEREFORD TIMES LTD., PRINTERS.

ten in 1956. In 1961 the Society sang Alan Bush's *The Winter Journey* Op. 29, a cantata for soprano and baritone, mixed chorus with accompaniment for string quintet and harp or piano, written in 1946. Cook also performed the *Seven Sea Poems* by Tony Hewitt Jones, written for Hewitt Jones's teacher in Oxford, Bernard Rose, and first performed in 1958. Two of the poems set are by the Ledbury-born poet John Masefield, 'Port of Holy Peter' and 'A Wanderer's Song'. In Richard Lloyd's first concert there was Hewitt Jones's *Good Company*, and in 1968 he conducted Christopher Brown's *Hymn to the Holy Innocents*, which was written in 1965 when the composer was twenty-two years old. Mathias's *This Worldes Joie* was sung in 1990 and 2003. But members of the Choral Society have been able to sing new music regularly in the Three Choirs chorus.

Not all of the singers sang in the festivals; volunteers offered themselves for an audition especially for the Festival Choir. Singers who weren't members of the Choral Society could also audition for the Festival Choir. Most of these had sung in past seasons with the Choral Society. In recent times auditions were held before the festival at Hereford which would allow a singer to take part not only in the forthcoming festival but in the next two festivals as well, the ones at Gloucester and Worcester. As Sinclair explained at the 1904 annual general meeting, the festival class was for the especially talented singers, the 'really good and efficient members of the society'.[10] They had to have good voices but, just as important, they had to be able to learn a good deal of music quickly. They had to be able to take time off work during the festival and so to have understanding employers as well as flexible and tolerant families. In the last decade there've been typically about two dozen chorus rehearsals in advance of the festival, half of which are full practices, two of which are all-day rehearsals. During the festival itself there would be daily rehearsals, morning or afternoon before the concert later in the day.

Because of the practical difficulties the largest choral contingent was usually from the festival city of a particular year. The challenges were clear enough: in 1902 the chorus sang *Messiah* and *Elijah* as they always did – though the Hereford Choral Society itself hadn't sung *Messiah* since 1884 nor *Elijah* since 1868 – but also a new work by Granville Bantock, *The Witch of Atlas*, and one by Walford Davies, *The Temple*. The fact that singers from Hereford had sung *Gerontius* at every previous festival since 1927 must have certainly have inspired confidence in the Choral Society members when they prepared for their own first performance in 1937.

The performances of Bach's Mass in B minor at the festivals at Hereford in 1924 and in 1927 undoubtedly assisted the preparation of selections from the work at the spring Choral Society concert in 1930, and the performances by the Festival Chorus at Gloucester in 1931 and Worcester in 1932 the performance by the Hereford Choral Society in 1933.

Repetition in both Festival Chorus and in the Choral Society must have eased the mastering of musical and vocal difficulties and increased the pleasure too that was derived from performing the same work. The Choral Society sang selections from Bach's *St Matthew Passion* in the spring concert in 1947 and the work was sung complete at the Gloucester festival later that year. It received festival performances in 1948, in 1950, at Hereford in 1952 and then by the Hereford Choral Society complete for the first time in 1954. Oc-

casionally it was the Choral Society which sang a work first: it sang Berlioz's *L'enfance du Christ* for the first time in 1950, which work was not sung at the Three Choirs until 1952 at Hereford.

The opportunity of singing in the Three Choirs Festival certainly offered a much wider scope of activity and some greater challenges to the Choral Society's singers than the choir's own concerts. Singers in the Festival Chorus were able to sing important works that had never been presented by the Choral Society: Stravinsky's *Symphony of Psalms*, for example, was first sung in 1955, the *Canticum Sacrum* in 1963, the Mass in 1972. Mahler too has never been sung by the Hereford Choral Society; the Third Symphony, the Eighth Symphony – the 'Symphony of a Thousand' – have both been sung at recent festivals. And the Festival Chorus has been able to tackle a lot of new music including festival commissions from composers quite different stylistically, musicians like Francis Pott, Francis Grier, Judith Weir, David Briggs, Andrew Gant, James MacMillan, John Joubert, John Adams and Anthony Powers.

In the last three decades audiences at the Choral Society's own concerts have varied between about 350 and a thousand. The largest audience in that time – and probably the largest in the Society's history – was the 1004 that attended *The Dream of Gerontius* in March 1984. There were almost a thousand for Beethoven's *Missa Solemnis* at the Society's 150th anniversary concert. Otherwise it has been *Messiah* that has guaranteed high audience figures. But *Messiah* is a musical and social phenomenon in England which places it in a category all by itself. In 1904 a performance of Handel's *Alexander's Feast* was very well attended, and Sinclair noted that 'old Handel could still attract and delight a large proportion of the Hereford public'.[11] But a hundred years later it seemed Handel's name alone was not a big draw. A national publication, *The Organ*, saluted Hereford's 'invigorating reading' of Handel's 'rarely performed' *Judas Maccabaeus* in March 2004, with the conductor's 'exemplary' pacing and flow, the 'fine line-up' of soloists, which included Lucy Bowen, David Gould and Andrew Carwood, the 'splendid' chorus who 'respond with an admirable balance of musical skill and enthusiasm', with the three continuo players better than the reviewer had dared hope.[12] And yet this and the performance of *Israel in Egypt* in March 2002 attracted among the smallest audiences. And Mendelssohn too isn't the sure-fire hit with audiences that might be expected. *Elijah* is quite popular; *St Paul* in 2009 had the lowest audience figure in recent times, 361. Less well-known works do affect audience figures: Bernstein and Honegger, Rossini, Howells and Rutter, Ireland and Mathias, Duruflé and Poulenc, all attracted lower audiences.[13] To some it must have seemed, as it seemed to a journalist in Exeter in 1913, that however advanced the views of the organising committee of a choral society might be, they had to bear in mind business considerations, cling to conventions, and annoy 'the moderns'. They had to remember that the tried and tested exercised a magic spell over most of their public who enjoyed music 'for the sensuous pleasure it gives, irrespective of intellectual or technical features'.[14] Perhaps there were actually some of the singers interested only in 'sensuous pleasure' too. But that was in 1913.

At any rate there has remained a core audience and, in grant-giving local council terms, the Choral Society certainly constitutes a flourishing local organisation, and not – under normal circumstances – a candidate for bailing out.

Orchestras and soloists

The little band of the Philharmonic Society gave a concert in College Hall at Christmas in 1853. How would their playing have struck a twenty-first-century audience? They played Herr Ferdinand Wallerstein's 'Castle Green Waltz' as well as several Rossini and Auber overtures, and in the opinion of the *Hereford Journal* their renditions on this occasion were 'in a very superior style'.[15] This reveals a little about the relationship between players and critic, perhaps, but not so much about their competence.

The band for *Judas Maccabaeus* in May 1878 consisted of twenty-one players. There were seven violins, two violas, two cellos, two double basses, two flutes, one clarinet, two horns, one harmonium, one piano, drums, twenty-one players in all. The usage of the harmonium isn't clear. Maybe it took the organ's role and the piano the harpsichord's, a bold attempt at authenticity. Johnny Arkwright from Hampton Court is there among the fiddles with Mr Lambe, the solicitor to the Hereford Cottage Improvement Society, The Revd Rawlins with Mr Burville the two violas, The Revd Brown one of the flutes, Mr Bezant the jeweller again, this time on the clarinet, and members of the Heins family, who own the music shops, with Nicholas, who once sang in the Chapel Royal, there on the piano. But in 2012 the Choral Society performed Verdi's *Requiem* with the Philharmonia, certainly one of the best of all British orchestras, with a world-wide reputation. How was this transformation effected from a band of local amateurs to a symphony orchestra of international renown?

Hereford has always suffered from its remoteness. Elgar told Ivor Atkins, Sinclair's young assistant in Hereford in the 1890s, that there were more opportunities of hearing music in Worcester than in Hereford, for in Worcester, besides the amateur players, there were a number of professional musicians.[16] However, in 1888 a Gloucester musician named E G Woodward established the Herefordshire

Orchestral Society, which was made up of amateur players from the county and was later directed by Sinclair and then by Percy Hull. Its 'usefulness and efficiency' were saluted in 1913[17] and up to the 1930s it seems to have been this orchestra which provided many of the players for the Choral Society's players. In April 1899 the orchestra playing in the Society's performance of Gounod's *Faust* was composed partly of amateurs and partly of professional players from London[18] and this seems to have been the pattern over many years. No doubt contacts established during the Three Choirs Festivals were particularly useful in booking players from the capital. In the late 1920s attempts were made to find additional wind players in Birmingham, Cardiff and Bristol but these weren't always successful.[19]

Into the early 1920s the orchestra was still designated 'band,' the concerts given by 'Band and Chorus'. Then in the later 1920s it became 'Chorus and Orchestra'. For *King Olaf* in March 1931, it was 'Chorus and Orchestra of 250'. When the Society began broadcasting in the 1930s – there was a transmission of Coleridge-Taylor's *Tale of Old Japan* in March 1932 and of Part I of *Elijah* in April 1932 – the schedules announced 'Chorus and Orchestra of the Hereford Choral Society' in some papers and 'Hereford Choral Society and Orchestra' in others. The coming of the BBC made conditions both better and worse: worse in that the players in the BBC's own orchestras were contracted full-time and were not allowed to play in other orchestras at all, which reduced the available pool of professionals living in these centres, but better when the BBC stipulated an existing orchestra for a broadcast. Hereford then didn't have to build up its own orchestra for the occasion.

These 1930s broadcasts were part of a scheme devised by the BBC in Birmingham to work with choral societies around the Midland region. There were broadcasts by the Gloucester Choral Society, Worcester Festival Choral Society, The William Woolley Choral Society in Nottingham, the Derby Choral Union and the Birmingham Festival Choral Society. After a few broadcasts the music director at Birmingham held a meeting in May 1935 for representatives of the chief choral societies in the Midlands, of which Hereford was counted one. One of the points the BBC wished to discuss was the quality of orchestral playing. Several good choral broadcasts during the previous year, they told the choral societies, had been marred by 'indifferent orchestral playing'. The BBC now made it a condition that the City of Birmingham Orchestra was used rather than a local orchestra.[20] So it was the City of Birmingham Orchestra that was heard in the Society's broadcasts of Parry's *Ode for St Cecilia's Day* and Stanford's *Songs of the Fleet* in 1936, *Gerontius* in November 1937 and *Caractacus* in November 1938.

HEREFORD
CHORAL SOCIETY

FOUNDED 1837

SHIREHALL

On Thursday, March 7th, 1940

AT 2-30 P.M.

(TO END ABOUT 4-15 P.M.)

C A R M E N

(BIZET)

MICAELA	....	....	....	....	WINIFRED RADFORD
CARMEN	....	....	....	....	ASTRA DESMOND
DON JOSÉ	....	....	....	....	JAN VAN DER GUCHT
ESCAMILLO	....	....	....	....	LEYLAND WHITE

FULL CHORUS & ORCHESTRA

Principal 1st Violin .... NORRIS STANLEY

Conductor - Dr. PERCY C. HULL

TICKETS : *(numbered & reserved)* 5/- & 3/6, unreserved 2/-

The Plan may be seen and seats booked at Messrs. HEINS, Broad Street.
Unreserved also from A. C. Miller, Newsagent, St. Peter's Street.
Tickets available at reduced rates to parties and schools on application
to the Hon. Secretary : Mr. P. G. ARROWSMITH, 15 Bridge Street.

---

billed as 'Full Chorus and Orchestra' or else the Midland Symphony Orchestra, a broadcasting group whose personnel were largely also players in the City of Birmingham Orchestra (which in 1948 became the City of Birmingham Symphony Orchestra).

In December 1950 for Berlioz's *L'enfance du Christ* the Kalmar Chamber Orchestra was used, a London-based group of freelance musicians. In the 1950s it was the Albert Webb Orchestra, or the Albert Webb String Orchestra, or often the orchestra playing would 'include the strings of the Albert Webb Orchestra'. Albert Webb was a violinist and managed a Midland-based orchestra which broadcast frequently in the late 1940s and '50s on the BBC Midland Region. From 1970 to the early years of the twenty-first century the Orchestra da Camera was used almost exclusively. This orchestra was founded in 1957 – its inaugural concert was in September that year in Birmingham City Art Gallery. It became a non-profit-making charitable body in 1959, administered by a board of directors, some of whom have been conductors of the orchestra. The players are solo and chamber musicians living in the Midlands and it has been the ensemble used by a great many choirs and choral societies from Exeter to Lincoln and from Norwich to St Davids.[21]

From 2006 the orchestra for nineteenth- and twentieth-century works has been the Hereford Sinfonia, a scratch orchestra made up of players from Welsh National Opera, the BBC National Orchestra of Wales and local freelance musicians. For Bach and Handel the orchestra has been since 2005 a specially fixed ensemble, Marches Baroque, playing on eighteenth-century instruments or modern copies.

For special occasions there have been famous guest orchestras, including the City of Birmingham Symphony Orchestra for the performance of *Gerontius* in March 1984, marking the fiftieth anniversary of Elgar's death. The Royal Liverpool Philharmonic Orchestra played for the 150th anniversary concert in November 1987 in the *Missa Solemnis*, and the Philharmonia for the 175th anniversary in 2012 in Verdi's *Requiem*.

For soprano solos in the earliest decades one of the cathedral trebles might be used, or a local soprano like Miss Broad, or one of the Misses Cole from Tarrington. For soprano and mezzo-soprano or contralto solos it was often possible to engage young sopranos or contraltos eager for experience. At the Christmas Concert in January 1842 – 'a very rich treat'[22] – the alto solos in *Messiah* and in Crotch's *Palestine* were taken by the conductor, John Hunt.

At the performance of *Judas Maccabeus* in May 1878 the soprano soloist was Nessie Goode, who had recently graduated as a prize-winning student from the Royal Academy of Music.[23] Emily Squire, who sang at Sinclair's first concert in 1889, was a local girl,

---

What kinds of improvement this resulted in is impossible to judge fairly or accurately. But it's certainly evidence that there was a concern for raising standards, and we may be sure that the effect was to produce more polished performances. The dependability of the orchestra and its professional alertness most likely resulted in increased confidence among the singers too, with better attack and increased vitality. Through the war and in the years immediately after, the orchestra was either a scratch group and the performers

born in Ross into a musical family. Her father, who was a banker in the town, was a capable amateur violinist. One of her brothers was a violinist called Barré Squire, and another the very distinguished cellist W H Squire, much admired by Sir Henry Wood, who taught at the Royal College of Music and the Guildhall. He was a noted early interpreter of Elgar's Violin Concerto, which he recorded. Emily herself was educated both at the College and the Academy in London and in Paris, and first came to attention as a soloist at the Handel Festival in 1888. She sang as a soloist with choral societies in London and all over the country and at several Three Choirs Festivals.[24]

Alongside young professional singers in the 1870s and '80s would appear others who sang without a fee. The contralto in that *Judas Maccabeus* was Mrs Hargreaves Heap, the wife of the headmaster of the Hereford Proprietary School in Barr's Court,[25] 'who kindly gives her services' as she was billed on this occasion.[26] Sometimes such a soloist was referred to as singing *en amateur*. A singer might waive a fee because of a local connection or as a simple act of generosity, or to demonstrate that though she aspired to professional standards she wished to make clear her amateur status as an educated married lady who required no emoluments.

Who were the early tenor and bass soloists? In the earlier decades the Choral Society often drew on lay clerks in the cathedral choir or vicars choral of the cathedral to sing the solo parts. For the performance of Handel's *Samson* in April 1871 all three gentlemen soloists were vicars choral. Thomas Everett and John Taylor had recently arrived from Oxford where they had sung as choral scholars at Magdalen College, where Oxford Movement reforms were beginning to invest the worship with a new kind of intensity and John Stainer was beginning to effect a transformation of the singing. The third soloist was William Duncombe, that critic of the ladies of the Herefordshire Philharmonic who'd been at Brasenose College, Oxford and had read Literae Humaniores with modest success. But he'd also studied singing and harmony with the organist at Christ Church, Dr Corfe – Charles Corfe, a son of A T Corfe to whom John Hunt had been articled at Salisbury Cathedral. Even as an undergraduate he had earned a reputation as a soloist, making his debut in a performance of Mendelssohn's *Antigone* in Oxford in December 1853. He became an assistant vicar choral at Hereford in 1866. It was Mr Duncombe who conducted the Society in 1889 when the conductor was away getting married, and for many years he acted as secretary.[27] When Mr Duncombe appeared as a soloist at Tenbury in June 1863 to raise money for the restoration of a parish church, he sang Schubert's *Der Wanderer* 'in the most artistic manner', with 'the utmost feeling thrown into it', the *Hereford*

Times reported, and his performance of a German drinking song was 'most rapturously applauded' and encored.[28] In October 1866 in a miscellaneous concert in College Hall organised by the Choral Society his singing of *At Bacharach on Rhine* 'was received with quite a furore, and nothing but a repetition of the song would satisfy the demand of the audience.'[29]

The first part of Dr Sinclair's first concert with the Choral Society, in November 1889, was devoted to *Paradise and the Peri*, not the famous cantata by Schumann but a long forgotten one written in 1870 by the English composer John Barnett. The tenor soloist on this occasion was Mr C W Fredericks, who had been a lay clerk at Hereford between 1874 and 1884 and then left for Lichfield Cathedral.[30] He sang as a soloist with numerous local choral societies, including Worcester, Monmouth, and Gloucester, and he was 'a gentleman not unknown to Tamworth audiences'.[31] It was said that his singing was 'careful and correct', and he was clearly a reliable and intelligent musician. His voice was 'sweet' but it was small-scale, 'somewhat wanting in power'. The 'prolonged applause' though that he received at a performance of *The Creation* in 1881 was thoroughly deserved, the *Gloucester Citizen* reporter was sure. At least he did not display the 'vicious vibrato' to which the bass, Signor Ghilberti, inclined on that same occasion, which quality, 'however it may be tolerated in opera', seemed to the critic of the *Gloucester Citizen* 'to be out of place in oratorio'.[32]

The bass soloist in the performance of *Messiah* in 1905 was William Waite, the grandson of a singing teacher in Hereford. The tenor on that occasion was Henry Plevy, who was born in 1873 near the city, and in his early twenties farmed and played the organ in local churches and sang in the Choral Society. In 1898 he went to the Royal Academy to study singing and he later was a pupil of Sir Henry Wood.[33]

Only very occasionally indeed in later decades did a concert by the Society draw on local singers alone as soloists. It happened in 1958 when there was an urgent need to increase the Society's finances; the conductor proposed a *Messiah* be performed with the solos sung by with an outstanding chorister called Noel Davies and a new lay clerk, Nicholas Long, an alto who having lessons with the best-known countertenor of the day, Alfred Deller. Another Hereford lay clerk, Granville Lund, sang the tenor solos and a Gloucester lay clerk, James Walkley, the bass. But this was most unusual.

From Sinclair's time, from the turn of the century – when local singers alone began to constitute the Three Choirs' Festival Chorus – the Society became confident enough in its own abilities to seek out as a matter of course soloists who were experienced professional singers and could command an audience in concert-halls anywhere.

HEREFORD CHORAL
SOCIETY

FOUNDED 1837

"The Childhood of
Christ" *Berlioz*

THE SHIREHALL, HEREFORD
TUESDAY, DEC. 19th, 1950
at 7 p.m.

ENA MITCHELL   RENE SOAMES
GORDON CLINTON   DAVID FRANKLIN

FULL CHORUS AND ORCHESTRA
including a section of the KALMAR CHAMBER ORCHESTRA
Leader : HUGH McGUIRE

Conductor : MEREDITH DAVIES.

*NOTE.—This Concert is given with the support of the
Arts Council of Great Britain.*

SIXPENCE

wedding in 1922. Isobel Baillie was another; she sang in the broadcast of Elgar's *Caractacus* in 1938. Baillie and Suddaby were two of the sixteen distinguished solo singers for whom Vaughan Williams wrote his *Serenade to Music* in 1938 for Sir Henry Wood on his golden jubilee as conductor. Another was the tenor Heddle Nash, who sang in the Society's 1937 broadcast of *Gerontius* marking the centenary of the Choral Society's foundation. The contralto on that occasion was Astra Desmond, and Frank Phillips sang the two short bass solos, taking the place of an indisposed Arthur Cranmer at short notice. Frank Phillips later became familiar as a war-time radio news announcer.

Astra Desmond was one of the most highly-rated English contraltos of the early and middle decades of the twentieth century. 'Miss Desmond's voice has never sounded more serene in the Angel's music, and Mr Nash's more earnest in Gerontius's confessions of faith', said *The Times* in its review of that 1937 performance.[34] Kathleen Ferrier appears to have sung on only one occasion in Hereford Cathedral, in a Three Choirs *Gerontius* in 1952, just a year before she died.[35]

The soloists in Haydn's *St Cecilia Mass* and George Dyson's *Hierusalem* in November 1963 were Jennifer Vyvyan, Pamela Bowden, Wilfred Brown and John Shirley-Quirk, a quartet of exceptional distinction, but singers not untypical of the kind of artist the Choral Society was now able to attract regularly. All of them had particular reputations as oratorio singers, with frequent broadcasting and recording engagements, and they were active too as teachers. While the fees of solo singers might not match the eye-watering heights commanded by the nineteenth-century artists engaged for appearances at the Three Choirs Festivals,[36] still there were always tight financial restraints. In the later decades of the century negotiations might be carried out with concert agents responsible for the supply of a trio or quartet of soloists in a concert in an effort to reduce fees and administrative costs, like the Charlton Concert Agency or Singers Direct.

The most notable characteristic of so many of the soloists at the end of the twentieth and beginning of the twenty-first century was the number who had undergone training as choral scholars in university chapels. Of course many of the solo tenors and basses who had appeared with the Society throughout its history had sung with cathedral choirs. The tenor, René Soames, who appeared in *L'enfance du Christ* in 1950, sang in the 1930s in the choir of Westminster Abbey. The tenor David Galliver sang in the choir of New College, Oxford as an undergraduate in the late 1940s, and Gerald English, another tenor, sang for a time at St Paul's in the 1950s. The bass Roger Stalman sang at Salisbury in the 1950s. But in the past

The prestige bestowed by the broadcasting of some of the Society's concerts made it altogether easier for the very best soloists to be approached. Distinguished sopranos like Dorothy Silk and Elsie Suddaby now appeared with the Society. Miss Suddaby, a pupil of Edward Bairstow, the organist at York Minster, came back to sing at the last concert that Percy Hull conducted with the Society, in Edward German's *Merrie England* in 1949, which he had particularly wanted on this occasion as the Society had sung it on the eve of his

decade there's hardly been a concert of the Choral Society at which one at least and often two or three of the soloists hadn't held student choral scholarships, sopranos and mezzo-sopranos like Catherine King, Cecilia Osmond, Susanna Spicer – all at Trinity College, Cambridge – Julia Doyle at Caius, Cambridge, countertenors like Andrew Radley of Clare College, Cambridge, tenors like Andrew Carwood of St John's and Simon Berridge of Trinity, Cambridge, and basses like Jeremy Huw Williams of St John's. Several of the soloists had been cathedral choristers. The bass, Giles Underwood, had been a boy at Westminster Abbey and then a choral scholar at Magdalen College, Oxford. The tenor Simon Wall, who sang with the Choral Society in December 2012, was a treble at St Edmundsbury Cathedral, attended the Eton Choral Courses as a teenager and sang in the Rodolfus Choir, had a gap-year between school and university singing at Portsmouth Cathedral and was then a choral scholar at St John's College, Cambridge before winning a scholarship at the Royal Academy.[37]

New College, Oxford inaugurated a scheme in 1858 whereby over a few years all the lower parts in the choir would be sung by choral scholars, undergraduate members of the college. But by 1864 the college had decided the scheme had failed; few if any suitably qualified candidates were presenting themselves. The Provost at King's College, Cambridge over-ruled a proposal for undergraduates to 'assist in the choir' in 1873: singing in a choir was below the dignity of young gentlemen. He was himself overruled in 1881 though he forbade the expenditure of any college funds on them. They had to be provided for out of 'private liberality', which is how they were initially funded. Choral scholars were gradually introduced, but it was only in 1928 that the lower parts at King's were taken by choral scholars alone. Many of them went on to be ordained or to became schoolmasters; hardly any sang professionally afterwards until the 1950s. Only one choral scholar at King's College, Cambridge, Sir Steuart Wilson, went on to have a career as a solo singer before the Second War. Up to that time there were not many of them. It was only in 1949 that St John's, Cambridge used choral scholars exclusively without any older lay clerks, and only from 1960 that Magdalen College, Oxford did.

The creation of choral scholarships for women's voices began with the choir of Clare College, Cambridge, who included women's voices from 1971 and the choir of Trinity College, Cambridge from 1982. More and more colleges – and not only at Oxbridge – have assigned resources to the creation of expert mixed-voice choirs whose primary function is liturgical. In 1978 St Mary's Cathedral, Edinburgh became a mixed choir. Salisbury Cathedral was the first English cathedral to take girls, in 1992, and today about a quarter

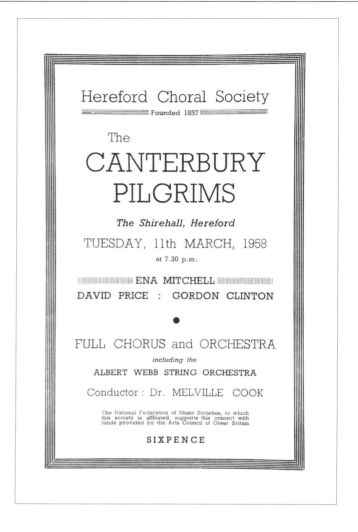

of choristers in cathedral choirs are girls. The emergence of a large number of professional singers who have sung as choral scholars has had a profound influence on the singing styles not just of the soloists but also of the choral societies themselves.

Standards and styles

During the Second War, when the Choral Society was contemplating giving a performance of *Elijah*, it was discovered that the Shirehall was not available, as it was being used to accommodate refugees. The choir's organising committee approached the Dean and Chapter, who, however, were not willing to give permission for a performance in the cathedral unless there was to be no charging for admission. They explained that they were contemplating a performance not by a full orchestra but by just organ and local string players and the solo singers too they suggested need not be artists of national renown, but good musicians recruited in Herefordshire. This attitude clearly stung members of the Committee and Percy Hull most of all. A reply to the Dean was prepared in the secretary's name but Percy Hull signed it; evidently Hull wished to make it crystal clear that the uncompromising views expressed in the reply were his own. The conditions that the members of the Chapter imposed would result in an inadequate performance, one which wouldn't reach the basic professional standards to which the Society now aspired, he told them. The BBC had been keen to broadcast their performances, which were also taken seriously by music critics on national papers. It caused evident hurt and surprise that those who had witnessed the choir's progress at first hand – the Dean had been at Hereford since 1919 – should set so little store by their recent achievements. At a time when there was an urgent need to foster the cultural life of the nation, the Choral Society deeply regretted that local music-lovers would be deprived of the opportunity of hearing an adequate performance of good music in the ideal spacious surroundings of the cathedral.[38]

The rising standards and growing ambition of the Society are not hard to trace. In 1895 Mr Duncombe, now the honorary secretary, considered that the Society's performance of *The Golden Legend* in April 1894 would have done credit to the choral society of 'any town in the kingdom', with the exception of the select few like Birmingham and Manchester. This was not just his opinion, he explained, but that of several professional men he had spoken to, 'not given to flattery'.[39]

In 1899 *The Musical Times* considered the singing of the Choral Society 'remarkable for freshness and vigour combined with delicacy and attention to light and shade'. Intonation and attack it considered 'worthy of the highest praise'.[40]

Reporting on the 1904 season in January 1905 Mr Duncombe, who'd been singing with the Society now for four decades, thought that to attempt *Caractacus*, as the Society had done that year, demonstrated its abilities as well as its 'laudable ambition'. He thought that the rich and massive scoring of such a work as *Caractacus* showed clearly though the need for more 'choral power', especially in the inner parts.[41]

By the later 1930s, with the BBC's insistence on high orchestral standards, the Choral Society no longer saw itself primarily as a 'class' for giving amateurs some experience at making music together but as a promoter of regular high quality public concerts. At the annual meeting in February 1924, Percy Hull referred to the popular French psychologist Émile Coué, a pioneer of auto-suggestion

---

HEREFORD CHORAL SOCIETY

SAMSON

Handel

Hereford Cathedral
(By kind permission of the Dean and Chapter)

Saturday, 17th March, 1973
at 7.30 p.m.

WENDY EATHORNE	MARK DELLER
(SOPRANO)	(COUNTER-TENOR)
KENNETH BOWEN	JOHN CAMERON
(TENOR)	(BASS)

JOHN SANDERS   ROBERT GREEN
(HARPSICHORD)   (ORGAN)

ORCHESTRA DA CAMERA
(AUGMENTED)

Leader : KENNETH PAGE

Conductor : RICHARD LLOYD

The National Federation of Music Societies, to which the Society is affiliated, supports this Concert with funds provided by the Arts Council of Great Britain.

PROGRAMME - - - - - - - 10p

---

with his mantra: 'Day by day, in every way, I am getting better and better.' Well, the Choral Society had no need of such a mantra. It was just plain fact: 'Each year and every year we are getting better and better.'[42] The singing of *Caractacus* in 1928 may have been 'magnificent' in Percy Hull's opinion, but the small number of tenors and basses was as ever causing great concern, and could easily lead to the end of the Choral Society. The ladies should form themselves into pairs and each pair should go out and bring in one extra gentleman member, if necessary 'by the scruff of the neck'.[43]

Three years later Mr Hull, who had after all been a member of the Choral Society since 1889, was sure that the performance of *Hiawatha* in November 1927 was 'the finest … choral singing by a long way' that had ever been heard in the Shirehall. He also reported – and it was not just local opinion, nor indeed national opinion, but the considered estimation of foreign experts as well – that the singing at the Three Choirs Festival at Hereford that year was judged to have reached the very highest standards. And the backbone of the Festival Chorus had indeed been formed by members of the host city's Choral Society.[44] In the spring concert of 1930 the Society sang the Mass in B minor for the first time – or, at least, selections from it – and Percy Hull was taken aback by the results achieved. He thought it was 'a wonderful performance'. Mr Sumsion of Gloucester and the conductor of the Bristol Choral Society, Mr Underwood, 'were astounded at the excellence of the chorus and orchestra'.[45] By now broadcasts and records were making it possible for audiences as well as singers in choral societies and conductors too to hear performances which were held at the time to be as good as any. And the critic of The [London] Times felt no need to make allowances for the performance of Gerontius in 1937. He considered the choral society at Hereford to be 'at a high pitch of excellence'.

And then there were the opinions of visiting soloists. Arthur Cranmer was a bass who made several appearances with the Choral Society between the wars. He was held in high regard by Vaughan Williams who spoke not just of the loveliness of his 'velvety tone' but of his 'sureness of purpose' and his 'artistic conscience'.[46] Illness prevented Cranmer singing in the 1937 Gerontius but he managed to listen to the broadcast and he wrote to Percy Hull: 'I should have considered it an honour to have been one of the performers ... I was so sorry to have let you down.'[47]

On the other hand the professionalism and reliability expected of a first-class choral society today may be more recent than is sometimes assumed. H C Colles, chief music critic of The Times from 1911 until 1943, wrote in 1942 that in 'our slipshod musical life it has become proverbial that a bad rehearsal means a good performance and vice versa. Never fully prepared, the semblance of preparedness which a lucky final rehearsal gives often leads to complacence in the subsequent performance, while a bad rehearsal puts everyone on their mettle to display their British phlegm. It is splendid, though it is not art.'[48]

One aspect of the singing of choirs has undoubtedly improved unequivocally in the recent past: tuning is far, far better than it was a century ago, even half a century ago, everyone seems to agree. This is the most striking difference that has struck Lindsay Lafford in recent visits to the Three Choirs Festival after a life spent abroad and mainly in the United States: choirs sing in tune, even unaccompanied choruses maintain pitch. This was not true when Mr Lafford was a Hereford chorister (he was admitted in 1922 at the age of nine).[49] In April 1935 Bristol Choral Society broadcast a programme of unaccompanied English music and the critic on the Western Daily Press was most impressed. This singing created 'a very favourable impression'; the programme had evidently been prepared with great care. 'The voices retained their vitality, resilience, and mellowness of tone throughout, and apart from an understandable drooping of the pitch at the end of Elgar's "My love dwelt in a northern land", there was nothing that one would have had otherwise.'[50] Very soon any 'drooping of pitch' in a live performance, let alone a broadcast, would not have been considered 'understandable' and not so easily forgiven.

The history of auditioning singers for the Choral Society is murky. Voice tests for membership in modern times were instituted in September 1982 'in the face of some opposition'.[51] The constitution in force in the 1980s and '90s refers to performing members of the Society being required 'to provide such evidence of musical ability as the Hon. Conductor may require'.[52] This suggests that the conductor might waive the test if he already knew the candidate for admission was a good singer. In 1989 the conductor said that he had been thinking about a possible retirement age for chorus members, though he'd not come to any firm decision.[53] In 1996 notice was given that 'existing members who joined before 1982 may be expected to audition at some point during the 1996/97 Season'. The conductor explained that he really did not wish to audition members who had sung for many years. He wondered if they 'might ease themselves out if they suspected they were not able to sing as well as they might once have done'.[54] In October 2006 the choir numbered 196, with sixty-five sopranos, eighty-one altos, thirteen tenors and thirty-seven basses. It was very awkward to fit 196 on to the platform. Balance of the parts was obviously difficult to maintain with such numbers, and crispness of attack very difficult to achieve. It was for these declared reasons that the conductor and accompanist decided that there should be voice appraisals for each singer every three years. The test would not be so difficult as the one for the Three Choirs Festival Chorus and vocal quality would be the deciding factor; sight-reading ability would not be so important.[55] All members wishing to sing in the Three Choirs Festival Chorus are required to attend an audition in the year of the Hereford festival, success in which allows them to sing in the festivals that follow at Gloucester and Worcester. It also obviates the need for a separate Choral Society re-appraisal.

But what of voice trials in the past? A local newspaper article during the Second War explained that 'the painful ordeal of a voice test etc, is absent'. Whether or not this was simply for the duration is not made clear. The article was clearly trying to encourage as many as possible to come forward and it holds out a further carrot: in peacetime, it explained, the Festival Chorus was recruited from the ranks

CLAUDIO MONTEVERDI

VESPERS
of 1610

Hereford Cathedral
(By kind permission of the Dean and Chapter)

Saturday
15th March, 1986
at 7.30 p.m.

❖❖❖❖❖❖❖❖❖❖❖❖❖❖❖❖❖❖❖❖❖❖❖❖❖❖❖❖❖❖

GILLIAN FISHER   **TRACEY CHADWELL**
(soprano)   (soprano)

TIMOTHY WILSON
(counter tenor)

ADRIAN THOMPSON   **CHARLES CORP**
(tenor)   (tenor)

BRIAN KAY   **MARK WILDMAN**
(bass)   (bass)

❖❖❖❖❖❖❖❖❖❖❖❖❖❖❖❖❖❖❖❖❖❖❖❖❖❖❖❖❖❖

HEREFORD CATHEDRAL CHORISTERS
HEREFORD CHORAL SOCIETY

ORCHESTRA DA CAMERA
Leader : KENNETH PAGE

DAVID BRIGGS - organ   **ROGER JUDD** - harpsichord

Conductor :   ROY MASSEY

The National Federation of Music Societies, to which the Society is affiliated,
supports this Concert with financial assistance from West Midlands Arts

of the Choral Society but because after a few months the conductor generally knows quite well the capability of each singer, there was no need for a test even for admission to the Festival Chorus.[56] This sounds as if it were a temporary expedient. When Elgar was living at Hereford in the 1900s he gave as his opinion – in the course of his Birmingham University inaugural lectures – that membership of a choral society should lapse after two years, or at least after three, when a re-trial must be held.[57] At that time candidates for membership were voted on by all the members, either openly or by ballot as preferred by the members. In the event of a ballot, a candidate would be excluded if more than a quarter of members were not in favour. All this was after a test with the conductor who had to be satisfied 'as to voice and musical capacity'.[58] There seems to have been no provision for regular re-auditions in the 1900s. The con-

flicting claims of friendship and high musical standards have clearly always been hard to resolve.

But what about the characteristics of the performing style? Is there, or has there been, a Hereford Choral Society *sound*? There is not much to go on. Twenty-five years after he had been to the 1904 Lower Rhine Festival, where he'd heard *The Apostles* performed, Elgar was asked about the differences between English and German choral societies. The Rhinelanders, he thought, lacked the North Country vigour and perhaps 'roughness' of Sheffield; they were more like a Three Choirs chorus, which a commentator in 1911 described as particularly distinctive, 'a choral ensemble of smooth beauty, especially luscious in the two upper parts, and carrying an exquisite, pure aloofness in sustained passages, but reaching its limitation in highly-coloured or dramatic music.'[59] One wireless listener to the Society's broadcast of *The Dream of Gerontius* in November 1937 enthused over the tone of the choir: 'The voices were so beautifully soft and round and absolutely true – no harshness anywhere.'[60] Smoothness and sweetness of timbre do seem to have been hall-mark qualities which have been detected over several decades.

In 1937 the critic from *The Times* noted the flexible tempos which Percy Hull gave to the music, how he would 'linger over significant moments and sweep over others in the onrush to a climax. The Demons' Chorus taken at a headlong pace was completely successful'.[61] This he put down to Hull's familiarity with Elgar's own performances which were characterised by a similar spontaneity and an improvisatory immediacy. Elgar himself insisted that his music should be played 'elastically and mystically'.[62] A *Musical Times* reviewer in 1926 thought that 'things which other conductors carefully foster, [Elgar] seems to leave to take their chance … At the end we realise that details and rhetorical niceties have been put in their right place, and that the essential tale has been vividly told.'[63] Hull certainly could be impetuous at times; he was criticised for taking choruses in the Mass in B minor too fast, for whipping up his singers, for allowing excitement to get the better of him.[64] But in Elgar, Percy Hull did indeed succeed in following the essential features of the composer's performances and, the experts agree, in catching their spirit. That much at least can be said from the fifty minutes of the Choral Society's 1938 broadcast of *Caractacus* that have miraculously survived.[65]

By the 1930s, though, Percy Hull too, and not just Elgar, belonged interpretatively to an earlier age. In 1929 the critic from *The Times* exhorted the Gramophone Company to record Elgar directing his works since 'his mind, especially in the oratorios, moves in a region for which notation offers no precise record … Posterity should be told exactly how Sir Edward Elgar meant his music to sound'.[66]

A century of recordings has demonstrated that interpretations are constantly changing, that there can never be any consensus about a 'definitive version' of any musical work in the West European tradition. The nature of the notation that stimulates variety is one of the chief peculiarities – some would say glories – of the tradition. Posterity doesn't play Elgar as Elgar did, and never will.

The trends in twentieth-century performance styles were to interpret the score much more literally, and to sing and play in a much tidier, neater style, with note values exactly observed and for there to be much less flexibility in tempos. So the Choral Society sang differently in the later twentieth century than it did in the earlier decades because of general anti-romantic tastes and aesthetic movements. There were also the huge influences of broadcasting and recording, which themselves encouraged accuracy and literalness. There was also the effect of the 'traditional' performing style of the English cathedral choir. This very distinctive style as it was known in the later decades of the century was in fact, in its most valued qualities, a new style. And because of technology – the long-playing disc – one choir was known above all others. And the choir that encapsulated the performing style of the cathedral choir wasn't even a cathedral choir.

A member of the Huddersfield Choral Society felt that the precise ensemble that that choir achieved in the 1980s and '90s owed much to the chorus master who was appointed in 1984, and that he derived this quality from his work as a member of the King's Singers, the six-voice group of men which gave its first professional concert under the name in 1968.[67] But the characteristics of the King's Singers' style originated at King's College, Cambridge, where most of the early members had been choral scholars and where similar *ad hoc* groups of King's choral scholars had been formed for many years to give performances in undergraduate concerts. The style was essentially that of the choir at King's, trebles with choral scholars, and it was a style that was taken at the time as representing the quintessential English cathedral tradition, though it was of recent origin. As with all performing styles, it is shaped by many factors. The discipline and blend derived from attitudes about the importance of being 'team players' and of self-effacement, and stemmed in part from the relationship between singers and director. It owed much to the temperament and personality of the choirmaster. In the 1960s the conductor was a senior member of the university and the men were junior members. Some of them at least would not just sing for their choirmaster, but be taught and assessed in formal university examinations by him. This was a quite different relationship from that which existed between lay clerks and choirmaster at King's, or indeed at cathedrals, eighty years before. The performing style

was, in other words, intimately related to the social and moral and spiritual worlds in which singers and conductor were living, as all performing styles inevitably are.

It quickly became well known through broadcasting and, especially, through long-playing discs. It had developed since the 1880s with the introduction of the first choral scholars singing with middle-class boys. The last lay clerk at King's had died in office in 1928.[68] It was from then on quite unlike any other choral foundation, where older lay clerks and not young choral scholars were employed. It represented a transformation in cathedral singing, and was highly influential because of its distinctiveness and because it was clearly musical expertise of a very high order. The lightness and brightness and the absence of any pronounced vibrato became a sound of 'early music'. It became a model, whether conscious or unconscious, of emerging professional choirs singing English sacred music in concert. The Sixteen and The Tallis Scholars both originated in Oxford, where the choir of Magdalen College was similarly constituted with choral scholars alone from 1959 (though they did sometimes listen to recordings of the Cambridge choir in Oxford at that time).[69]

It crucially informed the style of a choir whose conductor did not like the sound and style of King's, the Monteverdi Choir, who wished to avoid what he took to be its hallmark qualities. But as the membership of such a new kind of professional body depended on the expert disciplined young voices provided by the pool of ex-choral scholars now available, many of them from the King's College choir and all of them trained to observe similar technical and aesthetic ideals, the sound and style of King's moulded such a choir too. So that although this choir paid more attention to the colouring of vowel sounds and attempted greater stylistic contrast between different repertories, for example, its origins were not obscured. Not only foreigners recognised in its performances what they considered a quintessentially English style. This 'cathedral sound' moulded by King's College and Magdalen in the 1960s was developed by the choirs of the choral foundations into an idiomatic style too not only for 'early music' but also for twentieth-century composers like Stravinsky in his *Symphony of Psalms* or his Mass or the *Canticum Sacrum*.

So it is unsurprising that cathedral organists, who had been educated in a world which recognised the best college choirs as representing some kind of ideal in performing style, should encourage the cultivation of similar qualities in their choral societies. Nor were they pushing their society members in a direction in which they didn't wish to go. Many of the singers had known this singing style all their lives and counted its defining stylistic features as virtues and saw no reason not to emulate them.

The Choral Society has generally favoured maturer voices. Young families clearly have always limited the leisure time of parents and made a commitment to regular weekly rehearsals difficult to sustain. But the choir has continually welcomed younger singers and done its best to encourage them. In the 1880s, for example, it's possible to identify among the members a handful of teenagers or young people in their early twenties. There were the two young daughters of William Wigley, a solicitor's clerk living in Park Street. Percival Bulmer, son of the Vicar of Credenhill, was a member at that time. Now there was a young man in a hurry.[70] Music was clearly beginning to catch the interest of ambitious young men quite prepared to struggle into Hereford each week along muddy roads in mid-winter. Though perhaps it was Mary Herbert, the daughter of the Dean, who had caught Mr Bulmer's interest too. And there were the three Edwards girls, Florence, Minnie and Emma, the daughters of Augustus, the draper and milliner in High Town.

In the 1880s some members of the Society were not designated by voice-part in the registers but by the term 'elementary'. These were not all teenagers; some were married ladies. And there was Mr and Mrs Savory, living in Commercial Street; they were in the 'elementary' category and she was in her early forties and he must have been approaching sixty. In the Herefordshire Philharmonic Society at this time the conductor introduced his rule whereby new singers should not sing in a concert at all in their first year unless they attended every single practice.[71] Perhaps at some periods singers in the Choral Society were required to serve some similar kind of probation. And then there were those students at the Training College who were taught by Percy Hull.[72] The rehearsals in those days were on Fridays. There must have been a certain excitement at being allowed down town on a Friday evening, and you could probably be slightly ambiguous about why *exactly* you were going out.

There was a good reason, though, why young men should not be given too much encouragement to sing out vigorously. For the first century of the choir's existence there was a consensus among cathedral choirtrainers that the greatest care must be taken with the voices of young men during adolescence. One of the most famous trainers of voices around 1900 – he was in charge of the choir at St Paul's between 1888 and 1916 – was sure that a boy whose voice was changing 'ought no more to be allowed to sing than a man with a fractured limb ought to be permitted to walk or use it'.[73] For at least twenty years after choral scholarships were introduced for undergraduates at King's College, Cambridge in 1881, they were open to candidates 'not more than' or 'under 25 years of age'.[74] It was largely through the work of Sir Sydney Nicholson, who demonstrated in the public schools' festivals he organised at Gloucester during the

Second War and then the summer vacation cathedral courses of the School of English Church Music – from 1945 the Royal School of Church Music – that sixth-form boys showed that they could sing cathedral services to a very high standard. In 1945 *The Times* considered the 'modern theory … that boys should go on singing when the change of voice occurs' had been vindicated by his work.[75]

Nowadays the singers in Hereford's sixth forms, boys and girls, are so busy in their own school choirs as well as with their academic work that it would be difficult for many of them to become members additionally of the Choral Society. But evidence of the vast shift in attitude and rise in standards can still be glimpsed in the choir. The Cathedral Chapter established an organ scholarship in 2008 and three choral scholarships in 2010 for musicians in a gap year between school and university. These have all been required to join the Choral Society. But characteristically they've been cathedral choristers, music-scholarship boys to their senior schools, attenders at the Eton Choral Courses, members of the Rodolfus Choir, some of them already holders of university choral and organ scholarships: they can hardly be considered 'beginners'.[76] They have grown up in a world which values musical accomplishment very highly and is not suspicious of musicians as likely to be 'unmanly', of dubious morals, and intellectually challenged, the commonly-held attitudes of Victorian England.

In his Birmingham University lectures – delivered when he was living in Hereford – Elgar conceded that among soloists there might be 'some brainless singers amongst us still'. But he saluted choral singers in England who had 'long been our great insular wonder and pride.' In England, especially in the North, it was possible to have enough voices to draw on to achieve perfect balance, 'to turn out a machine as regular as a steam engine and perhaps as explosive. Every detail, every syllable is studied'. In recent years, he said, English choruses have been trained, 'perhaps over-trained in some instances … to a perfection of finish and attack never before attempted.'[77] Why did Elgar feel that some choruses had been 'overtrained'? His was a nineteenth-century, quintessentially romantic view of expressivity; he valued above all spontaneity. He wanted eloquence. He wanted projection. He wanted the gestures of the performers to reveal the narrative of the music, with inflections like those of a narrator unfolding his story for the first time. Until recent decades, character, individuality and eloquence were perhaps valued more than the understated smoothness and technical infallibility valued by the musicians themselves as well as the music-lovers of more recent decades, who have lived all their lives listening to recorded performances.

When Elgar's recorded performances were re-issued in 1957 to commemorate the centenary of his birth – they hadn't been kept in the record catalogues as historic performances are now – they were greeted with dismay. How could the composer and his performers have been so 'unmusical'? Commentators found it difficult to distinguish between technical competence and characteristics of a performing style: Elgar's performances were 'flawed', this soloist 'adopts' an 'exaggeratedly portamento style',[78] that soloist 'overdoes' portamento and rubato.[79] Certainly Elgar did not expect others to ape or copy his own performances. When he listened to John Barbirolli's 1928 recording of the *Introduction and Allegro* he noticed differences from the way he himself did things. But he knew, he said, that 'Mr Barbirolli is an extremely able youth and, very properly, has ideas of his own'.[80]

As more and more forgotten old recordings have been re-issued, we understand a little better how evanescent not just a live performance is but a recorded performance is too, since the style of the performance is the style, if not of the moment, then of an epoch. Styles of speech and physical gestures change, as we all know from old films and newsreels. Microphone and camera have reduced the size of physical as well as speech gestures.

The timbres and phrasing and speeds and ensemble of the music-making that was heard when the Choral Society appeared in All Saints' Church on Tuesday 12 October 1841 would not quite suit us.

The appearance of Miss Maria B Hawes, as she stood up to sing this masterpiece of melancholy heart-broken music ['He was despised'], was strikingly in character with its solemnity – her pale classic cast of countenance, collected manner and simplicity of attire, were all in harmony with the subject. Of her mode of delivery it is difficult to give anything like a description. There is a quality in the tone of her voice, and a peculiarity in her enunciation, verbal as well as vocal, which admits of no comparison with any other singer we ever heard – it is the combined result of deep feeling and fine intellect. There is a beautiful severity in her style, and a depth in both her conception and delivery, which place her beyond the reach of rivalry. Could Shakespeare be set to music, Maria Hawes should be the person to sing it. Throughout the whole of the piece, the congregation hung in almost breathless attention on her singing – anything more exquisitely touching we never heard – her intonation was faultless, her execution masterly … We must, on no account pass over the admirable mode in which the choruses … were sung by the choristers and members of the Choral Society; the points were all well taken up, and the most creditable precision observed throughout; nor must we omit to notice the commendable, and so far as we observed, solitary, example of Miss Hawes, in strengthening the effect of every chorus with her voice, which, like a strong-winged bird, easily clove its way through all the surrounding sounds, to the extremity of the Church – an example the good taste and good feeling of which other singers would do well to follow: it is well appreciated by the public.[81]

There's much here that we can't begin to imagine about the sounds and style. But much too that tells us that we do not share – cannot share – the good taste and feeling of the members of the Choral Society and its audience in 1841. Because the timbre of voices, tone colours, blend, balance, the quality of a crescendo, the particular manner of enunciating consonants, characteristic phrasings and articulations, all such details are components of a musical style which is itself part of a constellation of values, and not just aesthetic ones but also social and spiritual and moral ones.

As the violinist Carl Flesch used to say: 'There is something even more agreeable than beauty, and that is change.'[82] And as the conductor Roy Massey used to say: 'There is nothing as dead as the last concert'.[83] Though we have our memories.

Percy Hull

**The twentieth-century conductors
Percy Hull, Meredith Davies, Melville Cooke, Richard Lloyd,
Roy Massey and Geraint Bowen**

Sinclair, according to one of his choristers, 'chopped us up very fine'.[84] Which chorister was then apprenticed to him and became his assistant organist and accompanist to the Society and eventu-

ally his successor at the cathedral and as conductor of the Choral Society. Percy Hull was a child of the Choral Society – both his parents sang in it. He attended his first rehearsal in the spring of 1889 when Dr Colborne was away getting married and Mr Duncombe was taking the class. Percy Hull was small and, some thought, not very robust. But he survived four years as a prisoner of war in Germany at Ruhleben, which is perhaps some kind of indication of his resilience. His abiding characteristic was energy, both nervous and physical. He was an early riser. He was always in a hurry. When he wrote pencil annotations to a memorandum, the lead almost went through the paper. He was blunt and could be brusque. He was not too good at delegating. He liked being busy and he was impatient. But he was better than almost anyone else at solving practical difficulties of all kinds. Difficulties to him were, a friend once said, 'as gorse bushes to a bull-dozer'. He was psychologically astute as well. He enjoyed the exhilaration of conducting. He enjoyed rehearsing. He was clear and decisive in verbal instructions to large choirs and orchestras as in his physical gestures to them. Choruses enjoyed being ordered about; soloists didn't enjoy it but they unfailingly obeyed him. In a work such as Gustav Holst's *Hymn of Jesus*, with its rhythmic and metric complications, his firm and emphatic and utterly reliable beat made what had seemed impossible triumphantly possible. In the days when rehearsal time for the Three Choirs Festival Choir was ridiculously limited he steered his forces to safety when nearly all about him had been imagining disaster. Two evenings a week he would he would tear off on his bicycle to the Training College to give singing lessons, and especially musical students would be encouraged to sing in the Choral Society.[85]

Percy Hull was trained, as had been generations of cathedral musicians before him, by means of an apprenticeship with a cathedral organist. The only unusual aspect of his career was his spending the whole of his life in the precincts of a single cathedral. He was succeeded by Meredith Davies, whose advancement in the organist's profession was a characteristic one in the second half of the twentieth century. For it was indeed now a profession. John Hunt had been considered by university men *pleb*; Meredith Davies was himself a university man. He was the son of an Anglican clergyman. As a boy he attended the junior department of the Royal College of Music, and before he went to university he acted as organist at Hurstpierpoint College. He held an organ scholarship at Keble College, Oxford, and because it was not yet possible to read for a first degree in music at Oxford in the 1940s, he took a degree in Politics, Philosophy and Economics as well as a music degree. His war service in the Royal Artillery perhaps made his appointment as organist at St Albans Cathedral in 1947 at the age of twenty-five less surprising than it might otherwise have been. Sir David Willcocks served in the army during the war as an undergraduate, and on graduating he too was immediately appointed a cathedral organist, at Salisbury. Davies came to Hereford in 1950 – the year Willcocks went to Worcester.

Davies was taking over from Hull, who was seventy-one; Willcocks at Worcester was taking over from Atkins, aged eighty-one.

Meredith Davies

They were new men in a post-war world and it was a world in which new ideas on historical performance were being tried out by men like Thurston Dart, Anthony Lewis, Gerald Abraham and Denis Stevens. Such men worked in universities where undergraduate music courses were being established for the first time, and all four were also actively involved in broadcasting. Dart, Lewis and Stevens were also all distinguished performers, and Abraham a journalist. The history of music was being researched more energetically in England than ever before and the BBC Third Programme and the long-playing disc were providing new opportunities for the presentation of old music in performance, and for experiments in historically-informed performing styles.

Meredith Davies's first concert at Hereford was *Messiah* with a smaller orchestra than was then usual and, playing the harpsichord, there was Watkins Shaw, a teacher in Worcester and Librarian at St Michael's College, Tenbury. Watkins Shaw's 1959 edition of *Messiah*, which became widely used, took into account the details of eighteenth-century performing styles and had an incalculable effect on performances of the oratorio everywhere.

At the 1952 Three Choirs Festival in Hereford the harpsichord replaced the grand piano as the continuo instrument in *Messiah* and the *St Matthew Passion* – played by Boris Ord from Cambridge – and Alfred Deller, who was making frequent appearance on the BBC Third Programme, was the countertenor soloist in Purcell's *My beloved spake* and Bach's cantata *Erfreute Zeit im neuen Bunde* BWV 83.[86] During his time at Hereford Davies was drawn more and more to conducting, and he went twice to the Accademia Nazionale di Santa Cecilia in Rome to study conducting with Fernando Previtali. He was certainly aware of international standards of singing and playing, and the kinds of practical approaches that modern performing organisations demanded in order to reach them. And he was aware too of musical styles and idioms beyond the Anglican cathedral tradition.

When he was preparing in 1952 for his first festival as director at Hereford, he had been aware, he said, that the 'nascent festivals at Edinburgh and Aldeburgh were setting standards and winning musical prestige which could leave the Three Choirs looking like a very old-fashioned amateur junketing – as indeed, some critics were beginning to suggest'.[87] At Davies's first Three Choirs Festival, in 1950 at Gloucester, there had been one day's rehearsal for *The Creation*, the first performance of Finzi's *Intimations of Immortality* – to be broadcast – Holst's *The Hymn of Jesus*, the Fauré *Requiem*, Bach's *St Matthew Passion*, Howells's *Hymnus Paradisi* – also to be broadcast – the *Missa Brevis* of Kodály, *Messiah* and *The Dream of Gerontius*. *Messiah* was allocated five minutes rehearsal. A tenor asked what the dynamic would be for 'And with his stripes'. Gloucester asked Worcester, who did it *forte*. Hereford said they started quietly but got louder as the movement unfolded. Gloucester arbitrated: 'We'll sing it *mezzo forte*'.[88] In discussions long into the night after the 1951 and 1952 festivals, Willcocks and Davies planned far-reaching changes in rehearsal schedules, which they realised at Worcester in 1954 and at Hereford in 1955. Essentially they demanded more time with rehearsals close to actual performances. Davies left Hereford for New College, Oxford but after three years there he devoted himself entirely to conducting, his abilities being drawn to national attention in 1962 when he conducted at the first performance of Britten's *War Requiem* during the opening festivities of Coventry Cathedral.[89]

Meredith Davies was succeeded in 1956 by Melville Cook, whose training had been of the older variety. He was a chorister at Gloucester under Brewer – where he took part in performances directed by Elgar – and then as an articled pupil to Herbert Sumsion and later his assistant, during which period he also was organist at All Saints', Cheltenham, where Gustav Holst's father had been in charge of the

Melville Cook

music. Before he came to Hereford, he was, for nearly twenty years, director of music at Leeds Parish Church, with a choir of 30 boys and 26 men, and conductor of the Halifax Choral Society. It was his smartness and neatness that you noticed first when he walked about at Three Choirs Festivals, and his sartorial elegance reminded some festival-goers of his one-time composition teacher Herbert Howells.

Meredith Davies had endeavoured to bring Benjamin Britten to the Three Choirs, but dates could not be arranged in 1955. Britten did appear though at Melville Cook's first festival in charge, at Hereford in 1958, when he played the piano for his *Canticle II* and conducted the *Sinfonia da Requiem* and his cantata *St Nicolas*. *St Nicolas* Cook then did with the Choral Society in 1962 and he included the 'Choral Dances' from *Gloriana* in a concert in 1965. He also introduced works by Alan Bush – *The Winter Journey* and *In Praise of Mary* – and Kenneth Leighton's *The Birds*. At the Three Choirs he introduced Leighton's *The Light Invisible* in 1958, Fricker's *Vision of Judgement* in 1961 and Milner's *The Water and the Fire* in 1964. He was a wonderfully gifted keyboard player, very accurate, not given to display – he played Mozart piano concertos in

Richard Lloyd

reserve, rather distant manner and very disciplined rehearsal techniques were sometimes misconstrued as evidence of a lack of personal concern for his singers. But he had learnt his music and his behaviour too through the gestures and mannerisms of Sir Herbert Brewer. Brewer belonged to the generation of cathedral organists who had emerged from the lowly ranks of artisan performing musicians to become men to be reckoned with inside the cathedral itself and in the wider community they served. Perhaps they did take themselves a little too seriously. But they had worked in communities who until very recently had often seemed reluctant to take them seriously at all.

Musicians had had to banish the associations of effeminacy that still clung to music-making, to demonstrate their manliness. As the organist of New College, Oxford had insisted in 1918: 'The virtues of a good choir are very closely allied to those of a good regiment'.[90] And another characteristic quality of Melville Cook, his reticence, was a key component of the cast of mind of the men who formed the Oxford Movement, 'that reserve, or retiring delicacy, which exists naturally in a good man', as one of the leaders expressed it.[91] Like other conductors in the Choral Society's history he was unsparingly energetic. He didn't run marathons like Mr Bowen,[92] but he did walk the five miles from his home to Leeds Parish Church and back twice each Sunday. In choristers his mercilessly high standards could inspire both fear and reverence. By adults he was much loved and admired wherever he went. In 1992 he was invited back to Leeds Parish Church to read the lesson at their carol service that he had read fifty-four years before.[93]

And then in 1966 came Richard Lloyd, who had taken the commonest route to the post of cathedral organist in the later twentieth century. He was a cathedral chorister at Lichfield, organ scholar at Jesus College, Cambridge, and an assistant organist at Salisbury, where he had conducted the Musical Society and the Orchestral Society. A lay clerk who arrived on his departure was stopped in his tracks by the musicianship and discipline of the choristers, with the kind of blend and sweetness characteristic of the boys then at King's College, Cambridge.[94] Richard Lloyd was 'successful, popular and much loved'.[95] His Choral Society rehearsals were orderly, kindly and encouraging. But after he left Hereford he never directed a choral society again.

The organist of Hereford Cathedral must be a choir trainer, an organist, an administrator, a teacher – of children, of professional lay clerks, of orchestral musicians, of amateur musicians – and a diplomat with the wide-ranging negotiating skills required when working with personalities as varied as deans, vergers, organ tuners, probationer choristers, solo tenors and members of ecclesiastical

Society concerts – though his interpretation of Bach's organ music was considered at the time 'old-fashioned' in both registration and articulation. He had, after all, first heard Bach at the hands of Elgar and Sir Herbert Brewer.

He had private doubts about Anglican worship. Intellectually and instinctively he was ecumenical in religious outlook and he left Hereford for the New World, where he became an organist in the United Church of Canada, an amalgamation effected in 1925 of the Methodist Church in that country with the Presbyterians and Congregationalists. He was for many years organist at the Metropolitan United Church in downtown Toronto, which had a five-manual Casavant, the biggest organ in Canada. When, at the end of his life, he returned to live in Cheltenham, he became a Quaker.

He was said to be bitterly disappointed later in life when his

Roy Massey (2013)

AGM in February 1970 it was suggested that it be requested of the Chapter that concerts be held on Saturday evenings. Permission was given, though 'in the teeth of strong disapproval by the vergers',[96] and from November 1971 every concert has been held on a Saturday. In February 1971 the Chapter asked that a notice be placed in every programme to the effect that all performances in the cathedral be received without applause. Current convention dictated that there be no applause but not everyone was aware of convention. So there would often be a faint ripple of applause at the end of a concert and then an embarrassed silence, or giggles.[97] But not everyone accepted convention; there were even singers who did not accept convention. The '60s had, after all, come and gone, and in the 1970s the public could not always be relied upon to do what they were told. It was clearly the fault of the conductor – quite obviously the man in charge – if there was applause or there was not applause. But what should he do?

For many years concerts in the cathedral were held at the east end of the nave in front of the chancel steps. There was no raked staging. If you were short you would try to reserve a seat where you could see the conductor by placing your copy of the music on a chair in the afternoon. But if you were a short singer and unable to attend the afternoon rehearsal you probably would be able to see little if anything of the conductor.

Beginning with the concert of March 1973, the two major concerts each year were staged at the west end of the cathedral, which necessitated turning the pews around before each concert and afterwards, before the Sunday services.[98]

Would the boys from the Cathedral School be able to undertake this?
No, not on this occasion. There's an away match and two extra rehearsals that weekend for the school orchestra.

What about the Boys' Brigade?
The Boys' Brigade has disbanded.

The Venture Scouts? They did an excellent job three years ago.
The master-in-charge of the Venture Scouts has broken his leg and can't supervise them.

The Sea Scouts?
Will the Sea Scouts know how to turn the pews round?

But they're nearly all confirmed members of the Church of England: of course they'll know how to turn the pews round.

committees. If the cathedral is very lucky he might also be a composer, which Richard Lloyd was, having written all kinds of choral music, mostly for liturgical use. His heart was clearly in composition, and he certainly relished music-making of all kinds. But cajoling others to carry out the tasks necessary to support choral society performances was probably not an aspect of the job that appealed to his particular sensitivity. The chair of committee meetings from 1920 until 1969 had been the conductor. But from that last year another member of the committee served as chair and Richard Lloyd was probably relieved to be divested of this role.

There were still many problems in which the organist had to be directly involved. When Mr Lloyd arrived concerts took place on Thursday evenings with a rehearsal with orchestra on Thursday afternoons, which most of the chorus were unable to attend. At the

Roy Massey rehearsing in the Shirehall in November 1987

Who will give them a key?

They'll be supervised.
Can the concert manager supervise them without a verger?

But there will be a verger.
No there won't, not if it's after 11 o'clock.

But they'll have started by 11 o'clock.
Yes, but they won't have finished until after 11 o'clock.

Does the concert manager know that he's only able to switch certain lights on after the verger's left?
Yes. By the way, the concert manager can't supervise at all if the assistant organist is practising his Christmas voluntaries.

Why not?
Well, he can't if it's Messiaen.

Why not?
He can't guarantee that all the pews will be all turned and in order if there's Dieu parmi nous *going on while he's supervising.*

At a committee meeting in 1989 the conductor announced that the weekly rehearsals were going to be extended to two hours.

Everyone looked at the secretary. The secretary pointed out that if the rehearsal time was going to be extended something would have to be done about the cathedral's toilet facilities.

Everybody looked at the conductor. The conductor agreed to look into improved toilet facilities.[99]

At any rate the duties of the conductor of the Choral Society are considerably more varied and more demanding than those in the contracts of many distinguished *maestri*.

Of all the conductors of the Choral Society Roy Massey is the only one to have been neither an assistant nor an apprentice to a cathedral organist nor an organ scholar. But he had the inestimable advantage of being the rehearsal pianist at the City of Birmingham Choir to one the most renowned choral conductors of the day, Sir David Willcocks, which duties began when he was a schoolboy. Dr Massey also studied the organ with Sir David. He was born in Birmingham and educated both at school and university in the city and organist at two churches there before being appointed Warden of the Royal School of Church Music at Addington Palace and organist of Croydon Parish Church. He was then organist at Birmingham Cathedral for six years before coming to Hereford in 1974.

Dr Massey has the advantage of a marvellously expressive face which can transform itself from menacing scowl to beatific smile with the turning of a page. And back again. He was always full of quips and teased everyone unmercifully.

'Let me hear you sing this, altos, with all your accustomed aplomb and poise'; 'That was horrible! Back to letter H; H for *Horrible*'; 'Can you de-lumpify it a bit, basses? It's a bit rural.'[100]

He successfully pushed and prodded his committee into obtaining new platform staging. He suggested black bow ties (in place of 'dark ties' – bow ties had been previously considered 'inappropriate' for cathedral performance) and red folders for the music. The audience had had to queue for seats on the night of concerts. Now most seats were numbered and reserved and ticket sales rose accordingly, and audiences began to spill over into the nave aisles.[101] On his retirement the members of the Choral Society gave Roy Massey grateful thanks for his 'patience, impatience, rude remarks, sarcasm, skill, enthusiasm and fun over twenty-five years'.[102]

He was succeeded by a former accompanist. Geraint Bowen followed a now familiar trajectory for the aspiring cathedral organist, chorister, organ scholar – at Jesus College, Cambridge, Richard Lloyd's old college – and assistant organist – at St Patrick's Cathedral, Dublin and Hereford. After his assistant's job at Hereford he

Geraint Bowen rehearsing with chorus and orchestra in November 2012 *Derek Foxton*

became organist at St Davids Cathedral before returning in 2001. So he knew the Choral Society very well before he assumed the conductorship because of his years as accompanist. He was a boy at Hampstead Parish Church, where the choir was directed by Martindale Sidwell, who had himself been a chorister at Wells Cathedral under Conrad Eden. As great an authority as Barry Rose, in charge of the BBC's broadcasts of Choral Evensong as well as himself a renowned choirmaster at Guildford, St Paul's and St Albans, considered the three outstanding church choirs of the 1960s and '70s to be 'King's with Willcocks, Peterborough with Vann and Hampstead with Sidwell'.[103]

Martindale Sidwell was a small bespectacled man who could speak clearly, quietly, and unemotionally, even when he was delivering an assessment not entirely flattering of his singers' efforts.

Sidwell's unsleeping attention to detail was a characteristic no-one who remained his pupil or chorister failed to develop for himself. His first full practice with the choir at Hampstead Parish Church lasted an hour and was devoted to a single task: the monotoning of the Lord's Prayer. Rather surprisingly perhaps, he remained choirmaster at Hampstead for almost half a century.[104]

What struck members immediately was the meticulousness of Geraint Bowen's rehearsals. They resembled rather in their concentration – clearly the result of very careful thought and advance planning though seemingly spontaneous and always addressing real difficulties or faults or errors – the practices of cathedral trebles. There was never a moment wasted in moving from a rhythmic difficulty in this phrase or passage to a tuning problem in that one or to the diction everywhere. Many cathedral organists cultivate rather different styles in rehearsing a choral society and the cathedral choir, being generally more informal and relaxed with adult amateurs. Geraint Bowen's approaches seem quite similar. And this concentrated approach, with no second let alone minute wasted, is not a breathless one, nor a tiring one, but – partly because everyone can see so clearly the progress being made – encouraging and energising. Another choirmaster famous for steadiness and thoroughness in rehearsal, for quiet intense alertness, is Stephen Cleobury at King's College, Cambridge, with whom Mr Bowen studied the organ. Though the temperature has indeed risen a few degrees on occasion recently when scrambling has been introduced.[105] Members of the choir sit not in voice-part sections but in SATB groups, one to a part, having to hold their own against all-comers, just to be certain that each member is note-perfect and immaculately in tune.

Such rehearsal technique, quiet and concentrated and fast-moving, relies upon an accompanist of the greatest skill and intelligence, and one with sufficient experience to anticipate every next move. Everyone recognises the value of the current accompanist, Peter Dyke, who has held the post since 1998. The rehearsal pianists have been saluted regularly – after rehearsals, in conductors' annual reports – not only for their keyboard skills but for their marvellous abilities to anticipate the conductor's next move or the absence of a move at the next entry of the second altos. But they often seem to have been taken for granted. There is no role of honour for the accompanists. The list of planned expenditure for 1935 begins with 'Singers' and 'Orchestra', and ends up: 'stencilling; stationery; hire of piano; accompanist; sundries.'[106] And yet the required skills are clearly prodigious. In penetrating the anfractuosities of conductors' minds they have one enormous advantage: almost all of them are organists and many have themselves been cathedral choristers and so have developed instinctive responses to the suggestion of a raised eyebrow or a flicker of anguish from the choirmaster. Many have themselves gone on to become successful directors of choral societies including the Chinese Choral Society in Hong Kong; the Diocesan Choral Society in Jacksonville, Florida;[107] Gloucester Choral Society;[108] Tamworth Choral Society;[109] Monmouth and Stroud Choral Societies;[110] and, two of them, of Hereford Choral Society.[111] The records of accompanists are incomplete but it may be that there has been only one female accompanist, an excellent alert rehearsal pianist after the First War called Molly Hake. Being so impressed with the value of the services she rendered as accompanist, the conductor at that time, Percy Hull, followed the old-established custom – as the Dean once put it – of going to a creditor to whom he owed so much and asking for just one thing more, namely, her hand in marriage.[112]

Percy Hull was reluctant to delegate administrative duties. This telegram was in connection with the performance of Verdi's *Requiem* in 1949.

Organisation

'The members come on Monday evenings to sing, not to bother with financial affairs', said the conductor at one AGM. 'However,' he went on, 'someone has to keep things in hand.'[113] Who did keep things under control? They were a remarkable set of people, gifted, energetic, no passengers, no yes-men, hard-working, cheerful, marvellous to behold and a force to be reckoned with, the Choral Society Committee.[114]

The Society was established by its first conductor and the earliest musical directors also seem to have been in effect the chief administrators. In notices advertising the Society in the 1860s, the Society's second conductor, Townshend Smith, is designated 'Hon Secretary'; he acted as secretary to the Three Choirs Festival too for many years. Like Townshend Smith, Percy Hull was a most energetic administrator. He dealt with the BBC in all the most important matters; he sorted out fees payable to the Performing Rights Society.[115] When a music publisher omitted to send orchestral parts for a broadcast concert by the Society with catastrophic effects, it was the conductor who dealt with the firm.[116] When the Dean and Chapter refused to allow the Society to charge for concerts in the cathedral during the last war – which ruled out professional soloists and orchestral players and so brought concert-giving to a temporary halt – it was the conductor who signed the official response to the Dean.[117] Later on chairmen and secretaries shouldered the increasing administrative burdens. A treasurer was always needed. So was a librarian. And even in 1970 the executive officers of the Society consisted of just a chairman, a secretary, a treasurer and a librarian. But by the annual meeting in January 1972 there were additionally publicity officer, Patrons' secretary, ticket officer, concert manager.[118] In 2012 there were fourteen officials: chairman and vice-chairman, secretary and assistant secretary, treasurer, ticket secretary, Friends' secretary, librarian, members' secretary, publicity officer, concert manager, programme editor, advertising secretary and sponsorship secretary.[119]

The Choral Society was not established to generate profits but simply to support itself as a concert-giving organisation. In exceptional times, though, the Society has made donations, sometimes from money raised through concerts. In 1917 £70 was given to the Red Cross and the St John's Ambulance societies. During the Second War, when the Dean and Chapter would not allow priced tickets for admission to the Society's concerts in the cathedral, collections were taken during the concerts and when the concert-giving expenses had been met, donations made to prisoners of war.[120]

The Society raised funds through members' subscriptions and through ticket sales. In existence from the nineteenth century right up to 1982 was the Patrons' scheme: a Patron paid a subscription and received two tickets for each of the concerts. This was replaced that year when The Friends of the Choral Society were formed. They are still in existence. Friends make an additional payment and receive priority booking, a discount on tickets and pre-concert refreshments.[121] The cost of membership of the Choral Society and the price of the tickets for its concerts have required a similar outlay in real terms throughout its long history. The best seats in 1871 cost 2s 6d, which represented 82p in 1971 when the best tickets actually cost 60p. Top price tickets in the 1890s were 4s. This represented about £12 in the 1990s, and indeed the tickets for the Monteverdi *Vespers* in 1999 were £12 and £10.50, with unreserved tickets at £6. Four shillings for the top-price tickets in the 1890s represented about £17.50 in 2010, when ticket prices ranged from £10 to £22. In 1897 the annual subscription for singing members was 6s or 30p, which represented in 2010 prices about £27 or £28 when members were actually paying £85. The conductor in 1897 did inform members though that this was the smallest subscription he'd ever known in any choral society.[122] In 1950 the basic subscription of a singing member was 15s or 75p. In 2010 this would represent about £70. The actual subscription was increased to £67 in 2003 and to £85 in 2009. But in considering ticket prices and subscription charges it's important to remember that most inhabitants of nineteenth-century Hereford had much less disposable income than those since the 1950s. In these later decades, of course, the inhabitants of Hereford had many more kinds of entertainment and edification on which to spend their disposable income.

It seems that in the earliest days, with the close involvement of the vicars choral, College Hall was used without charges being levied, neither for rehearsals nor for the concerts. The soloists then were amateur musicians, as were most of the members of the band. But from very early on professionals were drawn on for the band and for at least some of the soloists and, financial margins always being very tight, there have been times throughout the Society's history when embarrassed appeals had to be made to the generosity of these professionals. When funds were low in November 1882 a violinist from Malvern reduced his customary fee to £1.11.6 but had to remind the treasurer the next February that the reduction had been for one concert only and – could they please note this? – the fee was now back at £2.2.0. And the treasurer did duly note it down, and a further increase too in 1885 to £2.12.6. 'Says he'll play for us "if disengaged". Oh really? In such demand? Who does this Mr Elgar think he is?'[123] In 1890 when the Society's finances were 'languishing' – the secretary's description – the conductor acted in some kind of mediating role with a soprano soloist who, as a result, 'gave her services at considerably below her usual terms'.[124] But the charm and persuasive power of a conductor could not always be relied upon to melt the hearts of hardened professional musicians. In 1933 a debit balance was paid off through Percy Hull and his pianist wife organising recitals.[125] It's true that in the 1930s there was a new source of income, the broadcasts by the BBC Midland Region for which fees were paid to the Society. But broadcasting and 78rpm discs, as well as the rising expectations of audiences and higher performing standards everywhere, were raising the normal fees of all professionals.

In 1979, after several years of protracted negotiations, the Society achieved charitable status, the greatest immediate advantage being that members' subscriptions could be covenanted, allowing the Society to recover income tax.[126] As no members of a charity could receive payment for their duties, neither conductor nor accompanist – who received honoraria throughout much of the twentieth century[127] – could be designated members of the organising committee. Henceforth, rather curiously, they attended meetings by invitation as 'musical advisers'.[128] But it had always been occasionally necessary to remind members very gently who was in charge. In 1927 Percy Hull remarked in passing that the Society could not get rid of him – he was very sorry about this – but the cathedral organist was conductor *ex officio*.[129] And members, even members serving on the committee, took their places so long as they could 'satisfy the Conductor as to voice and musical capacity'.[130]

By the 1970s more strenuous efforts were required to balance the books. Many of the money-raising activities since then though have been as much social as economic: members wished to come face-to-face with the singers with whom they stood shoulder to shoulder at single-minded rehearsals. A Social Committee was formed in 1972, which became known after its bank account title, COMSOC, which title led some to conclude that it was really a Marxist-Leninist groupuscule intent on a *putsch* against conductors and other oppressive figures of authority. By 1974 the Committee was able to hand over £400 to choir funds. It organised wine and cheese parties, weekly raffles at rehearsals, grand draws, sales of books, gifts and cards, market stalls, charity shops, bottle stalls, coffee mornings. In 1975 it sponsored a money-raising concert by the Wandsworth Boys' Choir, making a profit of £70. In the 1979/80 season COMSOC raised over £1,000 for the first time, and in 1981/82 it raised £1,600.[131] The Committee lasted until 1998, and in its final decade raised over £20,000. In the 1995/96 season alone it raised nearly £5,000.[132] From within COMSOC emerged the Hereford Carollers, a little group who rehearsed weekly, gave money-raising concerts and sang services in local churches and occasionally infiltrated pubs and astonished regulars by breaking into song and passing round cloth caps for donations.

Some of the most successful fund-raisers for the Choral Society were auctions of promises in which goods or services were offered. There might be a voucher for ten-pin bowling; a tour of the BBC Hereford and Worcester station; meals at cafes, restaurants, bistros and bars; an appointment at a health and beauty salon; lessons in Italian; lessons in singing; legal advice in making a Will; a trip round the House of Lords; assistance with A-Level Shakespeare; ten pounds of home-made marmalade; a case of Herefordshire wine; fruit cakes, pullovers and tomato plants; a cream tea in a wild flower meadow overlooking the Black Mountains; a day's sailing from Milford Haven to the island of Skomer to see puffins, guillemots, fulmers, and kittiwakes; a one-hour body massage; a cartoon of the conductor; a day's trout fishing; a trumpeter for a wedding.[133] Such an auction took three months to organise and a subcommittee of four.[134] The 2001 auction raised £3,717[135] and the 2006 auction £3,800.[136]

Besides the fund-raising of members in recent decades, there were grants from the local authority, with small annual contributions and occasional grants from West Midland Arts and guarantees from the National Federation of Music Societies. In 1993 a grant of £3,500 was given by the Foundation for Sport and the Arts, which was founded in 1991 to direct money donated by The New Football Pools. This particular grant was sought because the Society hoped to be able to present several important works to Herefordshire music-lovers whose importance and beauty were incontestable, but

Geraint Bowen and Roy Massey examining the conducting score of Elgar's *The Kingdom* in June 2013 in the room at Plas Gwyn in Hereford in which the work was completed in 1906 *Derek Foxton*

whose drawing-power was uncertain. These included Arthur Bliss's *Morning Heroes*, Elgar's *The Spirit of England* and *Lux Christi*, and Finzi's *Intimations of Immortality*.

When the Society included in a 2001 programme another performance of Finzi's *Intimations of Immortality* with Parry's *Ode on the Nativity*, it was able to secure grants from the Garfield Weston Foundation, a philanthropic trust, and from the Vaughan Williams Trust, which exists to promote the work of young composers and music by neglected or currently unfashionable twentieth-century British composers.

For the March 2006 performance of *The Kingdom*, a work completed by Elgar in Hereford in 1906 but never performed before by the Choral Society, the total costs amounted to about £15,600, of which the largest slice was for the soloists and the orchestra. Ticket and programme sales were expected to generate about £7,000, and the Society's regular fundraising activities which were to include an auction of promises would also contribute. Grants were successfully applied for from The Elmley Foundation – a grant-making charity which supports the arts in the counties of Herefordshire and Worcestershire and derives from the Elmley family of Madresfield Court in Worcestershire – the Elgar Foundation and the Friends of Herefordshire Museums. The largest award came from the National Lottery under the Awards for All scheme. Such successful grant application required not only a detailed breakdown of costs of the particular event for which funding was being requested, but the formulation of precise aims in mounting the event in question and a clear knowledge of the Society's audience and its particular tastes. So an audience survey had to be organised in 2005 to assist in gathering such information.

In 2006 the Society was given money to purchase music stands by the Rowlands Trust, a charity supporting the people of Birmingham and the West Midlands counties, and in 2008 a sum from the Skinners' Company Charitable Trust towards the purchase of a set of lights for orchestra stands. In 2007 the Friends and Patrons scheme was extended to include 'Business Friends'. Up till then Friends or Patrons were individuals making an annual payment and receiving priority booking, a discount on tickets and pre-concert refreshments. Now there could be corporate Friends, and Metal Merchants UK Ltd, BBR Optometry and Rees & Co Insurance all agreed to become Business Friends from the beginning. In that particular season, 2007/8, there were additionally two major sponsors, Hereford Osteopathy Practice and the Royal Bank of Scotland.

So for the later decades of the twentieth century, the Society derived its income from the sale of tickets, the sale of programmes and the advertising in them, and from members' subscriptions, the subscriptions of the Friends, from grants, bank interest, covenants and fund-raising activities. The Society's expenditure was on the accompanying orchestra, the hire of concert venue and rehearsal space, the concert fees, the hire of music, the costs in erecting a platform, honoraria for conductor and rehearsal accompanist, performing rights, insurance, publicity and administration.

What other problems did the Society's administrators have to solve? There was occasional trouble caused by the high spirits of young men and maidens who had failed to join the Choral Society but insisted on creating noise and disturbances in the Close during performances. So the West Mercia Police had to be persuaded to patrol the cathedral environs.[137] There was concert dress: the conductor once proposed 'cheerful' instead of 'long and black' as a dress code which was immediately greeted with enthusiasm by the ladies. Difficulties, though, quickly became apparent: 'cheerful' would change as fashions changed. How could you guarantee that a colour choice would be available in five years' time? Would dresses constantly have to be replaced as particular colours lost favour? Were there 'cheerful' dresses that could withstand the low temperatures and icy blasts of the cathedral in winter? Some problems were like bindweed and never satisfactorily rooted out. Reports of brightly coloured and 'flashy' jewellery would re-surface, and alleged sightings of décolletage from the fourteenth row – and even from the south nave aisle if you stood on your seat – and superintendents of dress code were re-appointed to inspect members before they moved into

the public gaze.[138] There were reports of members of the audience attending Evensong before the performance and then remaining in the locked cathedral so that they could slip onto unreserved seats before the doors were re-opened. Meetings were arranged to discuss with the cathedral's vergers how to persuade the sinners to repent or at least to stop sinning.[139]

In the earliest times College Hall may have been used by the Society without charge. In 1894 the College gave notice that College Hall could no longer be used for practices and the County Council granted permission for the Shirehall to be used for rehearsals as well as for concerts. And so it long continued. In 1959, when the Shirehall was unavailable, a concert was given in the Garrison Theatre, Bradbury Lines. From November 1971 concerts were always given in the cathedral. The two main concerts have been staged at the west end of the cathedral since March 1973. The improvement in sound that resulted was at the cost of the additional task of turning the pews around before each concert, and re-turning them afterwards, ready for Sunday services. It was quite clear though that the chorus should be raked so that voices could be directed over the orchestra.

So drama blocks from a local school were used, and the men in the back row were poised on chairs set on tables. This seems to have been considered less dangerous than previous arrangements and was used for a few seasons. In 1975 it was decided that just too much power and nuance was lost by the lack of elevation of some voices and new staging was a priority. It took almost five years though before a suitable and affordable system could be devised. It was designed by a member of the chorus and built locally, at Ewyas Harold. The drawings looked very satisfactory and yet, at the very moment the designs were about to be approved, disaster almost struck as members teetered on their chairs again. This time it was at the revelation of the cost involved, an astronomical £1,515. A staging fund had to be launched. About half the sum had been raised when the staging was first used, in 1979, and breathing-space in generating the remainder was found through an interest-free loan negotiated with the National Federation of Music Societies.[140]

This was all highly satisfactory until the cathedral authorities informed the Committee that they were not able to retain the staging between concerts. There was just nowhere in the Close. Fortunately, this being the Hereford Choral Society, a farmer could be found who would allow the use of an empty barn which was ideal for the purpose. Except when foot-and-mouth disease broke out and, as the concert date drew closer, the area round the outbreak in which movement was restricted was extended further and further and nearer and nearer the barn.[141]

At least no-one looked at the conductor.

Elgar and Vaughan Williams

For the first three decades of the twentieth century Elgar was the dominating figure at the Three Choirs Festival. Between 1904 and 1911 he was resident in Hereford, 'a desirable place wherein to dwell', he told a journalist in 1906, who described it for his readers: 'a quiet old-world place … tramless … *sans* manufactories'.[142] He was a great friend of both Sinclair and Percy Hull and Society members who sang in the Festival Chorus sang under his baton on many occasions. Lady Elgar was certainly a fan of the Choral Society. She once wrote to him – or at least the *Hereford Times* claimed she did – that 'it would have done you good to have heard *King Olaf* with such a chorus.'[143]

At the festivals members of the Society had sung in Hereford Cathedral under the composer's direction *Gerontius*, *The Apostles*, *The Kingdom* and *The Music Makers*. They'd watched him there in full court dress at the Opening Service; they'd heard him at rehearsal, so unimpressed with their singing of the great outburst at 'Praise to the Holiest': *It wouldn't scare a mouse*. And then repeating it for him with such energy and vehemence and determination that the cathedral seemed to rock.[144] And they'd watched his arrestingly alive face and the earnest eyes, and waited for his features to light up with a smile full of emotion and gratitude and thankfulness when the music went well. They remembered how Elgar didn't command the musicians but implored them 'to give all the fire and energy and poetry that was in them'.[145] And *The Times* critic had listened to the Choral Society's singing *Gerontius* in 1937 with 'delightful freshness and buoyancy as though they had been singing it all their lives'.[146]

Elgar has surely been a continuing inspiration to members of the Choral Society. He walked these streets, he leant against these pillars, he listened to these very sounds on the cathedral organ. Great things, we all know, happen anywhere. But it's easy to forget this. Through natural modesty, perhaps, as well as through a lack of confidence in any gifts we may possess. Not *here*. Not *me*. But Elgar helps to remind musicians in Hereford that great music can be conjured up anywhere, and not elsewhere, but here on this very spot. *Rarely, rarely comest thou spirit of delight*. And so it must have sometimes seemed on a wet Monday evening in November in the rehearsal room. And the singers remember how often Elgar too became disheartened by the littleness of life. But then they remember that there, along the road to Mordiford, amongst the apple orchards by the Wye, were found out 'human feelings so nervous and subtle as … had never before spoken' in English music.[147]

In August 1836 an article appeared in the *Hereford Journal* wringing its hands over the lamentable state of cathedral music. The

Percy Hull, George Bernard Shaw and Edward Elgar cross the cathedral close.

government seemed intent on silencing choirs. The author of the article complained bitterly about the proposal of the Ecclesiastical Commissioners to do away with the colleges of vicars choral, like the one at Hereford. And at this moment of all times, when 'Popery [was] making such rapid advances in England, and cathedral-like structures [were] rising around us for the performance of mass, in which the aid of music will be called in to allure Protestants'.[148] Earlier that year the newspaper had alerted citizens to news from Birmingham that a cabal of Roman Catholic priests had perfected themselves in the Welsh tongue, produced a mass-book in Welsh, and were about to begin 'a Popish mission in the Principality'.[149] This was all in the aftermath of the Catholic Emancipation Act of 1829. And of course suspicions remained and divisions were clearly demarcated. Still, in 1920 – a century later – the Dean and Chapter at Worcester were directing that the name of the Mother of God be excluded from the text in a performance of *Gerontius*.

From its very foundation though, certainly from the beginning of the re-constituted Society in 1863, it was an ecumenical organisation, open to those of any denomination and of none. Elgar himself was a very obvious demonstration of the inclusiveness of the music-making in Hereford. As he put it in his letter to the Archbishop of Canterbury in 1927, congratulating Randall Davidson on the twenty-fifth anniversary of his becoming archbishop, he himself stood aside from the trivialities which inform the controversies between Protestant and Catholic. Whatever differences there might be, there remained, he knew, 'the clear, wide and refreshing Christianity, desired by all men, but obscured by the little darkness of their own imperfect vision'. He had tried to exercise his art to the better understanding of 'such broad Christian feeling'. And he offered to the Archbishop a 'tribute of deep respect' to a man who was 'an embodiment of all that is good and true in Christianity past mere forms and observances'.[150]

And then there was Vaughan Williams – a 'cheerful agnostic' – who had a profound effect on the music-making of all English choral societies and perhaps the one in Hereford more than most, through his music certainly, but through his words too, and the attitudes he embodied towards amateur music-making particularly. He was after all a familiar presence at the Three Choirs Festival. Herbert Howells never forgot the revelatory first performance of the *Fantasia on a Theme by Thomas Tallis* in Gloucester Cathedral in 1910, when he and Ivor Gurney afterwards paced the streets of Gloucester all night: 'It seemed so incredibly new at the time, but I soon came to realise how very, very old it actually was, how I'd been living that music long before I could even begin to remember'.[151] The next year the *Five Mystical Songs* were given their first performance at Worcester. In 1912 it was Hereford's turn with the first performance of *Fantasia on Christmas Carols*. He was an unforgettable figure, 'very tall, very beautiful' as a younger man, as Ursula Vaughan Williams described him,[152] and just as arresting a figure in the 1950s, in his eighties, padding about softly but majestically, nodding his old head like an owl.[153]

He was convinced of the crucial importance of amateur music-making in any community. Music was, 'above all things', he thought, 'the art of the common man',[154] 'above all others, the art of the humble'. He disliked the categorisation of music into popular and classical, the highbrow and the lowbrow, and longed to see the creation of 'an art in which all can take part'.[155] He thought that the greatest music had 'the element of popular appeal'.[156]

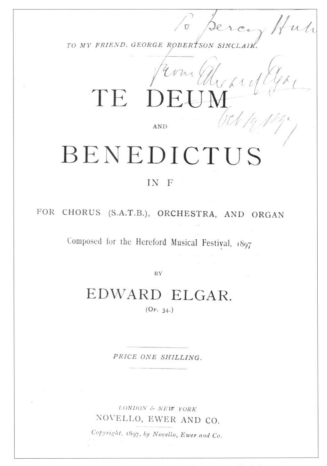

'It is very very modern, but I think it will do' was Sinclair's verdict on this work for the Three Choirs Festival after Elgar played it over to him and Percy Hull in his house in Church Street, Hereford on 5 June 1897.

The most serious music-making was not, according to Vaughan Williams, mere entertainment, although that's what *The Times* seemed to think, he complained, at least that's how it advertised performances of the *St Matthew Passion*, under 'Entertainments'.[157] It was not merely the creation of structures in sound projected and articulated by the performers. The sounds and structures of music in performance enabled those involved in the music 'to understand what is beyond the appearances of life'; music represented 'a reaching out to the ultimate realities by means of ordered sound';[158] music offered 'a vision beyond earthly sense'.[159] Intimacy, naturalness and spontaneity were prerequisites of the deepest musical experiences. So self-consciousness in a performer was death. Preoccupation with the 'correct' number of oscillations in a shake, or with its 'correct'

Vaughan Williams and Lindsay Lafford at Cornell in 1955. Between 1922 and 1935 Mr Lafford was a member of the Society as chorister, accompanist and tenor, and he also played second bassoon in the orchestra on occasion.

termination would kill spontaneity and naturalness and destroy any chance of that kind of vitality which was a *sine qua non* for genuine musical expression in Vaughan Williams's view.

He wanted to hear a flesh-and-blood creature speaking to other living men and women. He might have agreed with the recorder-player Frans Brüggen that a performance, a live performance, must have mistakes in it because they are a part of natural speech, of natural delivery to an audience.[160] Otherwise a performance becomes artificial, without character, too good to be true. He agreed with Parry that the beauty of the French horn derived partly from its 'human fallibility'.[161] And he would have understood Sir Walter Parratt, his organ teacher, who refused to descend from the organ loft at St George's Chapel, Windsor to direct the choir; some extra fine shading might have been attained, some greater precision in ensemble with a conductor, but these gains would be offset by the loss of spontaneity.[162]

Music-making was a corporate act involving both performers and listeners; the listener must be drawn up into the music, must be on the inside, not remaining on the outside as a critic, or a connoisseur, whether of compositional technique or performance expertise. The attitude of the listener should not be critical, or detached, or neutral, but expectant, ready to receive. The greatest music demands not cold, aloof impartiality, but imaginative sympathy, and emotional involvement by both performers and listeners alike. Vaughan

Williams spoke of listening to a performance of the Verdi *Requiem* when the music 'possessed' him.[163]

His well-known and often-repeated views on attempts to re-create eighteenth-century sonorities and performing styles and his suspicion of the early music movement of his time are usually taken as the dogmatic pronouncements of an old man whose tastes were formed in another age, through his experience of singing in the Bach Choir for sixteen years early in the century, and then conducting it in the 1920s, perhaps by the performances of the cantatas he listened to with such delight at the Sing-Akademie in Berlin in 1897. By the 1950s it could not but be otherwise that such a musician, however enlightened, open-minded and adventurous, would inevitably fail to appreciate how thoroughgoing investigations into historical styles were sweeping aside yesterday's clichés and revealing this music in startlingly fresh colours. Vaughan Williams could be forgiven his views, because of his age, and also because of his own creative genius, whose inevitable blind spots and prejudices were inseparable from his creative gifts.

But while such views were formed in part by taste, as they always must be, it is more important to realise that he was protesting so relentlessly over so many years – and, it must be said, with some degree of relish – not so much about sonorities and performing styles as such as about attitudes to music and the states of mind of those engaged in music-making, whether as executants or as listeners. Preoccupation with the precise realisation of the 'curlicues and twirligigs' of old music,[164] with a concern to reproduce expressive elements which were not part of a performer's habitual and natural expressive vocabulary, was not only likely to inhibit the performer but would also tend to lead to the creation of audiences of specialists, connoisseurs of the most minute inflections in articulation, artificially revived and only distinguished and admired by a handful of cognoscenti. Bach's masterpieces should be presented, as he put it in a famous phrase, 'to everyone – not only to the aesthete, the musicologist or the propagandist, but above all to Whitman's "Divine Average"'.[165] He considered great music as his friend the historian G M Trevelyan considered great literature, not as an intellectual conundrum, a puzzle to be solved or worked out by the application of rules; it was 'joy in our innermost heart. It is a passion like love, or it is nothing.'[166] 'The history of events is ephemeral, and for the scholar', Trevelyan said on another occasion; 'the poetry of events is eternal, and for the multitude.'[167]

Vaughan Williams' vision of music as a life-changing, life-sustaining, life-enhancing force, if in essence the legacy of the nineteenth century, is one that singers in choral societies are perhaps loath to abandon completely in the twenty-first.

The letter from Elgar's daughter, Carice, to Percy Hull after the performance of *The Dream of Gerontius* in November 1937.

Why did they sing?

Was it Vaughan Williams's vision that sustained them? Was that why the members of the Choral Society subjected themselves to the terror of a voice trial, the tyranny of the conductor, the discipline of weekly practices sometimes on cold, wet evenings and sometimes in cheerless rehearsal rooms?

Singing in a choral society was always supposed to be good for you. The *Hereford Journal* was sure in 1838 that choral societies 'expand the mind and improve the morals of those who might otherwise seek pleasure in less innocent amusements.'[168] The *Journal* was always a strong advocate of musical experience. Three years later it explained that 'turbulence of disposition and rudeness of manners can hardly subsist with a keen perception of the beauties of music'.[169] Sometimes there was great disappointment and disil-

lusionment. At Chepstow they'd formed their choral society and by 1849 it had one hundred members. Not only that, there were seventy members in the Young Man's Reading Society. And yet, even so, there remained 'a considerable portion of the population ... destitute of the tastes which such institutions are calculated to form and encourage.' There had been so little progress, the paper informed its readers sadly, so little mental and moral improvement in Chepstow, that they were having to establish an efficient police force.[170]

Perhaps you should not ask or expect too much even from rational entertainment. And if we're inclined to laugh, let us remember our own equally eccentric notions, that piping canned Mozart to babies, for example, will make them more intelligent.

At the annual meeting in February 1895 the Dean, who was in the chair, was impressed that so many had come to their rehearsal and had not used 'the inclemency of the weather' that week as an excuse

Society members rehearsing for the Three Choirs Festival 2013 in College Hall on 20 June that year *Derek Foxton*

to stay at home. He recognised, he said, the educational importance of the Society and he knew too that it was a gathering of friends.

When Canon Bannister, the Precentor of the cathedral, told members at the annual meeting in 1920 that he considered singing in the Choral Society to be 'an essential part of their higher education' – his remark was greeted with applause – something different was intended.[171] By 'higher' he clearly didn't mean advanced knowledge about music. Maybe it was more akin to the convictions of those early advocates of music appreciation who are often misrepresented as having as their goal information about sonata form and the instruments of the orchestra. In 1895 one of them insisted that

it was not enough for men and women to become learned in distinguishing between musical styles and periods, it was not enough for music-lovers to be able to describe and analyse formal procedures as evidenced in particular compositions; all this was as nothing unless music-lovers were 'steadily gaining in a vital, hearty, spiritual sympathy with composers and performers as representative men, and through them with the essential life of mankind'.[172]

Percy Hull told the Society at the annual meeting in 1920 that the members would find nothing under the sun to take the place of music. Many men went mad, he said, in his prisoner-of-war camp in Germany. Putting on plays helped keep men sane and playing games did too. But above all else it was music, making music and listening to music, that calmed and inspired and gave hope to his fellow prisoners.[173]

Regularity and punctuality were essential habits to cultivate and yet, Percy Hull thought in the 1920s, particularly difficult for young people, with counter attractions like tennis in the summer, dancing in the winter and films all the year round. In 1927 he talked of his great admiration for the fortitude of older members who set such a fine example to younger members in sticking to the Society and turning up to rehearsals and concerts.[174] Mr White, the secretary, saluted the 'positively heroic' attendance of some members who did not miss a single rehearsal neither of the Choral Society nor of the Festival Chorus during 1930.[175]

Enthusiasm though? Surely genuine enthusiasm arises spontaneously; you can't order people to be enthusiastic. But as a composer creates the conditions in which inspiration is likely to strike, so can the choral singer create conditions for generating enthusiasm. (The members can all turn up on time for a start.) And fortunately enthusiasm is very contagious. Elgar's daughter, Carice, wrote to Percy Hull after the 1937 Gerontius and told him she thought the chorus were marvellous. 'They seemed so unflagging after all that rehearsal in which they seemed to give all they had – and yet in the evening they still seemed to have it all to give and more – and what I loved was … the real love and enthusiasm they brought to it – as if it meant such a tremendous lot to them to be doing it.'[176] (The letter is reproduced on page 67.)

And friendship: Percy Hull told the Society that when he first returned to England after years in a prisoner-of-war camp he felt that the world was a very dull and dreary place and felt very old, but that since 1921, thanks to great support he had received from the Society, he felt twenty years younger.[177]

As when Ivor Atkins in 1922 told Elgar about his rehearsals of *The Kingdom* for the Three Choirs:

I cannot tell you what joy we have had in rehearsing it. It has brought back many memories, not only to me personally but to the older members. It has many hallowed moments and I find it very moving. We sing it intimately (when we are at ease) and all of us feel you very much in our midst. I don't quite know what it is about the work, but when I put it on for rehearsal we all feel a little different and as the music proceeds I grow tenderer towards them and they to me and we end up by being better for the music. It is a good feeling.

Ivor Atkins goes on to say that old associations and memories have something to do with it. But in addition there's a 'conviction of the oneness of us all which is unforgettable'.[178]

And 'the oneness of us all'. A listener at the 1937 *Gerontius*, a visitor from Oxford, said to her hosts afterwards: 'Wonderful, to sit for two hours on seats not too soft, in a Cathedral none too warm, and realise nothing but the Music, and the great joy of it.'[179]

In the sermon preached to mark the 150th anniversary of the Society's establishment, the Precentor examined Handel's claim that he would be sorry if he only 'entertained' an audience with his *Messiah*: 'I wished to make them better', he said. The Precentor concluded that in saying this he wished to suggest not just moral goodness. 'He meant he hoped his music would make us more human, more civilized, more liveable with; better able to handle our failures and our successes, with humility and gratitude; an inspiration to help us treat others with compassion and understanding, to live less selfishly, more generously and graciously'.[180]

When he left the Choral Society in 2001, Roy Massey agreed that they'd all had a lot of fun.[181] He meant *fun* surely as Noël Coward was referring to it when he said that work was 'much more fun than fun'. Psychologists say that people are happiest when they're least self-conscious, when they are so absorbed in an activity that they can forget themselves. To have to meet a challenge, a complicated mental and physical task, a corporate task that demands total concentration with everyone prepared and trained enough to make success a realistic possibility, such an activity holds out the promise of happiness.[182] That's what they say.

* * *

Christabel Hopton, who lived at Hampton Manor in Tupsley, joined the Society for the 1920 Worcester festival after the death of her young husband on active service with the 1st Shropshire Yeomanry. She went on singing until, in January 1948, she failed a voice test. She wrote to Sir Percy Hull to tell him how very greatly she'd enjoyed singing under his direction all those years. But she would still come and listen, she told him. Oh yes. Yes, she'd still be listening.

'I shall always endeavour to support the Choral Society and the Festival as much as it lies in my power.'

She hesitated. She was biting her lower lip.

Singing in the Choral Society, she said, had been 'one of the chief pleasures of my life'.[183]

Notes

Preface

1 Programme leaflets 1852–1904; HCA D865/4/1.
2 Printed booklet: *Rules of the Hereford Choral Society* (as revised on 2 February 1900): stuck into the Minutes Book 1891–1923; HCA D865/1/2.
3 Programme leaflets 1852–1904; HCA D865/4/1.
4 Programme leaflets 1852–1904 and 1845–2011; HCA D865/4/1 and D865/4/2.
5 Minute Books 1891–1923 and 1923–69; HCA D865/1/2 and D865/1/3.
6 Printed accounts for 1 October 1922 to 31 December 1923, Minute Book 1891–1923; HCA D865/1/2.
7 Letter to subscribers; HCA D865/2/9.
8 Registers and concert programmes 1923–7; HCA D865/2/4.
9 *Hereford Journal*, 13 June 1838, p. 3; *Hereford Times*, 16 June 1838, p. 3; 'Celebration of the Coronation of The Queen', *Hereford Journal*, 4 July 1838, p. 3.
10 Choral Society's scores; HCA D865/12.

Chapter I

1 *Hereford Journal,* 23 December 1835, p. 3.
2 *Hereford Journal,* 30 December 1835, p. 1.
3 *Bath Chronicle and Weekly Gazette,* 17 September 1829, p. 1.
4 *Hereford Times,* 15 February, 1845, p. 3; *Hereford Times,* 28 December 1844, p. 3; 'the Worcester Road': 'New-street' in St Peter's Parish in Hereford, today's Commercial Street, was known by that name for a short period in the 1830s and 1840s. See Ron Shoesmith and John C Eisel, *Pubs in Hereford City* (Little Logaston, 2004), p. 290.
5 John Locke, *Some Thoughts Concerning Education* (London, 1693), p. 235.
6 *Hereford Journal,* 30 December 1835, p. 1.
7 Jane Austen, *Pride and Prejudice,* Vol. I, ch. XVIII.
8 Letter from Ouseley to Stainer, no date, British Library Add. MS 62121, fol. 3.
9 Letters from Ouseley in Germany to Wayland Joyce dated 21 and 28 October 1851, in J W Joyce, *The Life of the Rev Sir F A G Ouseley* (London, 1896), pp. 76–8.
10 Lowell Mason, *Musical Letters from abroad: including detailed accounts of the Birmingham, Norwich and Dusseldorf Musical festivals of 1852* (Boston, 1853), pp. 12–13; pp. 309–10.
11 S S Wesley, *A Few Words on Cathedral Music* (London and Leeds, 1849), p. 72.
12 William Gardiner, *Music and Friends; or, Pleasant Recollections of a Dilettante* (London, 1838–53), Vol. I, pp. 282–3.
13 John Jebb, *The Choral Service of the United Church of England and Ireland: Being an Enquiry into The Liturgical System of the Cathedral and Collegiate Foundations of the Anglican Communion* (London, 1843), p. 112.
14 Unattributed undated sheet in Richard Okes's handwriting headed the 'United Universities Club, Pall Mall'; King's College, Cambridge KCAR/8/3/40.
15 Memorial to the Chapter from the College of Vicars dated 1 October 1865. Chapter Acts 7 November 1865; HCA 7031/21, pp. 224–8.
16 Injunctions or Statutes dated 10 November 1870; HCA 4459.
17 Letter from John Goss, Custos, dated 2 December 1873. College of Vicars Choral Acts; HCA 7003/1/6, p. 348.
18 Parliamentary Papers, 1883, xxi, p. 27; The Revd Douglas George Manning MA, Priest Vicar of Wells Cathedral.
19 See Ella M Leather, *The Folk-Lore of Herefordshire* (Hereford/London, 1912).
20 'Breaking up of the ice in the Wye', *Hereford Times,* 10 February 1838, p. 3.
21 'St Peter's Library', *Hereford Journal,* 14 February 1838, p. 3.
22 *Hereford Journal,* 12 April 1837, p. 3.
23 'St Peter's Reading Association', *Hereford Journal,* 30 October 30 1839, p. 3.
24 'Proposed Mechanics' Institution for the City of Hereford', *Hereford Journal,* 15 January 1840, p. 3.
25 'Ross Choral Society', *Hereford Times,* 30 November 1844, p. 3.
26 'Cricket', *Hereford Journal,* 2 May 1838, p. 3.
27 Quoted in Peter Bailey, *Leisure and Class in Victorian England: rational recreation and the contest for control 1830–1885* (London and New York, 2/1987), p. 54.
28 'Concert at the Shirehall', *Hereford Journal,* 30 July 1851, p. 3.
29 Chapter Acts, 10 November 1859; HCA 7031/20, p. 480.
30 *Hereford Journal,* 13 June 1838, p. 3.

31   'Celebration of The Coronation of the Queen. Hereford', *Hereford Journal*, 4 July 1838, p. 3.

32   *Hereford Times*, 27 October 1838, p. 3.

33   *Hereford Journal*, 5 December 1838, p. 3.

34   *Hereford Times*, 3 August 1839, p. 3.

35   'Herefordshire Society', *Hereford Journal*, 17 April 1839, p. 3; 'Herefordshire Society', *Hereford Journal*, 5 June 1839, p. 2.

36   'Laying the Foundation Stone of St Martin's New Church', *Hereford Times*, 10 October 1840, p. 3; 'St Martin's New Church', *Hereford Times*, 16 October 1841, p. 3.

37   'Anniversary of the Hereford Mechanics' Institution', *Hereford Times*, 6 March 1841, p. 2; 'Hereford Mechanics' Institution', *Hereford Times*, 6 March 1841, p. 3; 'Anniversary of the Establishment of the Hereford Mechanics' Institute', *Hereford Journal*, 10 March 1841, p. 3.

38   'Hereford Choral Society', *Hereford Times*, 6 June 1840, p. 2.

39   'Hereford Choral Society', *Hereford Journal*, 5 January 1842, p. 3.

40   'Musical Institution', *Hereford Times*, May 2 1840, p. 3.

41   'Hereford Philharmonic Society's Concerts', *Hereford Times*, 10 February 1844, p. 3. Handwritten concert programmes, 7 February 1844 to 9 June 1846; HCA D865/1/1 (at the back of the book).

42   D Lysons, J Amott, C Lee Williams, H Godwin Chance, *Origin and Progress of the Meetings of the Three Choirs of Gloucester, Worcester & Hereford and of the Charity Connected with it* (Gloucester, 1895), p. 15.

43   Minutes of meetings and copies of the rules of the Philharmonic Society written and printed; HCA D865/1 (at the front of the book).

44   For details of these vicars choral, see *Biographical Memoirs of the Custos and Vicars admitted into the College at Hereford from 1660 to 1823 – Collected from public records and private researches by a former member of that Society* by The Revd William Cooke, Vicar of Bromyard, Rector of Ullingswick and a magistrate of Herefordshire, died 18 October 1854; HCA 7003/4/4; for the Munseys see also http://herefordshire1757-1820.typepad.co.uk/herefordshire_17571820/2011/04/james-munsey-of-crown-sceptre-hereford-died-1827.html; accessed 15 December 2012.

45   Unattributed Preface in *Songs by the Late John Hunt, Organist of Hereford* (London: Cramer, Addison, and Beale, n.d.) (British Library gives 1843), pp. 9–10.

46   Cooke, *Biographical Memoirs of the Custos and Vicars*); HCA 7003/4/4.

47   Samuel Webbe (ed.), *Convito Armonico*, 4 vols (London, 1808–23). Printed volumes bound together into a presentation volume with the inscription 'Presented to the College Philharmonic Society, By the Rev J Jones 1838'; HCA R.8.3.

48   Minutes of the Philharmonic Society; HCA D865/1/1.

49   John Hullah, *The Duty and Advantage of Learning to Sing: A Lecture delivered at the Leeds Church Institution, February 19, 1846*, (2nd ed., London, 1846), p. 20.

50   *A selection of Favourite Catches, Glees, &c as sung at the Bath Harmonic Society, with the Rules of the Society, and a List of Members* (Bath & London 2/1799).

51   'Hereford Philharmonic Society's Concerts', *Hereford Times*, 10 February 1844, p. 3.

52   'Hereford Choral Society' *Hereford Journal*, 26 October 1842, p. 3.

53   'Hereford Choral Society's Easter Special', *Hereford Journal*, 17 April 1844, p. 3.

54   'Hereford Choral Society', *Hereford Journal*, 12 June 1844, p. 3.

55   James Brown and Stephen Stratton (eds.), *British Musical Biography: a dictionary of musical artists, authors and composers born in Britain and its colonies* (Birmingham, 1897); http://archive.org/details/britishmusicalboobrow.

56   'Concert of Sacred Music', *Hereford Journal*, 28 February 1846, p. 5.

57   'Concert', *Hereford Times*, 7 March 1846, p. 8.

58   'Hereford Musical Festival', *Hereford Journal*, 19 August 1846, p. 3.

59   'The Hereford Musical Festival', *London Standard*, 12 September 1846, p. 1.

60   'Hereford Choral Society', *Hereford Journal*, 5 April 1848, p. 3.

61   'Hereford Choral Society', *Hereford Journal*, 25 June 1851, p. 3.

62   'Hereford Choral Society, *Hereford Journal*, 3 March 1852, p. 3.

63   'Hereford Choral Society', *Hereford Journal*, 9 June 1852, p. 3.

64   'Hereford Choral Society', *Hereford Journal*, 9 June 1852, p. 3.

65   'Hereford Choral Society', *Hereford Times*, 28 October 1854, p. 8.

66   'Hereford Choral Society', *Hereford Times*, 28 April 1855, p. 5.

67   'Hereford Festival', *The Musical Times*, Vol. 7, No 151 (September 1855), pp. 107–8.

68   'Hereford Choral Society', *Hereford Times*, 1 November 1856, p. 8.

69   'The Hereford Choral Society', *Hereford Journal*, 16 June 1858, p. 5.

70   'Hereford Choral Society.-Concert', *Hereford Times*, 20 July 1861, p. 5.

71   'Concert of the Hereford Choral Society', *Hereford Times*, 26 October 1861, p. 8.

72   'The Hereford Choral Society', *Hereford Times*, 8 February 1862, p. 7.

73   'Presentation of Testimonial to G Townshend Smith, Esq', *Hereford Times*, 5 September 1863, p. 4.

74   'Hereford Choral Society's Midsummer Concert', *Hereford Times*, 25 July 1863, p. 8.

75   Under 'Haynes, Walter Battison' in Brown and Stratton (eds.), *British Musical Biography*; http://archive.org/details/britishmusicalboobrow.

76   *Hereford Times*, 25 July 1863, p. 8.

77   'Presentation of Testimonial to G Townshend Smith, Esq', *Hereford Times*, 5 September 1863, p. 4.

78   'The Earthquake', *Hereford Journal*, 10 October 1863, pp. 3, 8; http://www.geologyshop. co.uk/ukequakes.htm; accessed 13 January 2013.

79   List of 'performing members' given on the reverse of an 1863 programme sheet; Leaflets advertising programmes of the Society; HCA D865/4/1; personal details from *Littlebury's Postal and Commercial Directory of the County of Hereford* 1867.

80   Michael Kennedy, *Portrait of Elgar* (London, 2/1982), p. 140.

81   'Music, a Means of Popular Amusement and Education', *The Musical Times*, Vol. 3, No 67 (December 1849), pp. 240, 245.

82   'The Sayings and Doings of Cheltenham', *The Cheltenham Looker-On*, 20 December 1856, p. 1220.

83   *Herefordshire Portraits (Past and Present) Illustrated by Reproductions from Photographs of Herefordshire Men or Men Connected with Herefordshire* (Hereford: Jakeman & Carver, 1908), p. 49.

84   Letter from W D V Duncombe to J A Arkwright dated 7 August 1889 with an accompanying handwritten note beginning: 'I quite agree with JHA …'; Hereford County Record Office A63/IV/31/16.

85   Handwritten report for the 1891 season. Minutes of the General Annual Meetings and committee meetings from January 1891; HCA D865/1/2.

86 Printed leaflet, 'Report of the Hereford Choral Society for 1908'. Printed annual reports and accounts 1902–10'; HCA D865/2/2.

87 'Tea Meeting', *Hereford Journal*, 1 January 1845, p. 3.

88 Unidentified newspaper cutting annotated 'Feb 2 1917' reporting the Society's annual meeting. Minutes of the General Annual Meetings and committee meetings from January 1891; HCA D865/1/2.

89 G B Shaw, *Music in London 1890–1894*, 3 vols (London, 1932), Vol. 1, p. 80.

90 'The Hereford Choral Society', *Hereford Times*, 8 February 1862, p. 7.

91 'Hereford Choral Society', *Hereford Journal*, 12 June 1844, p. 3.

92 'Concert', *Hereford Times*, 21 November 1857, p. 5.

93 Peter Gay, 'The Art of Listening', *The Naked Heart: the Bourgeois Experience, Victoria to Freud* (London, 1995), p. 14.

94 Charles Burney, 'Essay on Musical Criticism', *A General History of Music from the Earliest Ages to the Present Period* (1789), 4 vols. (1776–89); two-volume edition, ed. Frank Mercer, 1935), II, p. 7.

95 Edward Elgar, *A Future for English Music and other lectures*, ed. Percy M Young (London, 1968), p. 61.

96 *The Three Choirs Festival 1952: Hereford Music Meeting*, 10 September 1952, in the cathedral. 'Book of words' for this concert (words and programme notes).

97 Anthony Boden, *Three Choirs: a History of the Festival* (Stroud, 1992), p. 143.

98 'Hereford Choral Society', *Hereford Times*, 1 November 1856, p. 8.

99 'Hereford Choral Society Concert', *Hereford Times*, 20 July 1861 (author's italics), p. 5.

100 *See* Tim Blanning, *The Triumph of Music: Composers, Musicians and Their Audiences, 1700 to the present* (London, 2008), pp. 28–9.

101 http://www.thebachchoir.org.uk/about/history.php; accessed 12 December 2012.

102 'We have seen the testimonials …' *Hereford Times*, 14 January 1843, p. 3; 'Mr G Townshend Smith … Begs to Inform the Inhabitants of Hereford …', *Hereford Journal*, 18 January 1843, p. 3.

103 'The Herefordshire Choral Society', *Hereford Journal*, 25 October 1843, p. 3.

104 Choir and Class Singing', *Hereford Journal*, 20 September 1854, p. 3; 'Mr W J Burvill … Teacher of Music and Writing', *Hereford Journal*, 29 October 1856, p. 2.

105 'Miss Paine … Professor of Music & the Pianoforte', *Hereford Times*, 2 February 1861, p. 4.

106 'Singing Class for Ladies', *Hereford Times*, 19 April 1862, p. 4.

107 'Manliness in Music', *The Musical Times*, Vol. 30, No 558 (August 1889), p. 460.

108 Francis Hueffer, *Half a Century of Music in England 1837–1887: Essays towards a History* (London, 1889), pp. 1–3.

109 See Catherine Beale, *Champagne and Shambles: the Arkwrights and the downfall of the landed aristocracy* (Stroud, 2006).

110 Herefordshire Philharmonic archive papers 1863–99; HRO A63/IV/30-33.

111 Beale, *Champagne and Shambles*, pp. 63–4.

112 Herefordshire Philharmonic Society, *Hereford Times*, 11 May 1867, p. 6.

113 http://wanderingminstrels.org/; accessed 19 June 2012.

114 Programme for a 'Vocal and Instrumental Concert in the Assembly Room [Hereford] on the 21st of January 1863'. Herefordshire Philharmonic Archive Papers 1863–99; HRO A63/IV/34/6.

115 Abridged notes of the Meeting of 9 July 1866. Herefordshire Philharmonic Archive Papers 1863–99; HRO A63/IV/34/3.

116 Note dated 22 December 1886 in H Leslie's hand; Herefordshire Philharmonic Archive Papers 1863–99; HRO A63/IV/30/9.

117 Letter from Henry Leslie to J Arkwright dated 28 December 1886. Herefordshire Philharmonic Archive Papers 1863–99; HRO A63/IV/30/9.

118 Letter from Henry Leslie to J Arkwright dated 20 November 1886; Herefordshire Philharmonic Archive Papers 1863–99; HRO A63/IV/30/9.

119 H Leslie to Arkwright, letter dated 21 November 1886; Herefordshire Philharmonic Archive Papers 1863–99; HRO A63/IV/30/9.

120 Unsigned and undated note: 'I quite agree with JH…'; Herefordshire Philharmonic Archive Papers 1863–99; HRO A63/IV/31/16.

121 Watkins Shaw, *The Succession of Organists* (Oxford, 1991), p. 267.

122 John Rouse Bloxam, *A Register of the Presidents, Demies, Instructors in Grammar and Music, Chaplains, Clerks, Choristers and other Members of Saint Mary Magdalen College in the University of Oxford From the Foundation of the College to the Present Time: Vol. I The Choristers* (Oxford, 1853), p. 215.

123 E H Fellowes, *Memoirs of an amateur musician* (London, 1946), p. 9.

124 For the history of St Michael's College, Tenbury, see David Bland, *Ouseley and his Angels* (Eton, Berkshire, 2000).

125 Preface, *Songs by the Late John Hunt*, p. 8.

126 'The Late John Hunt Esq', *Hereford Times*, 26 November 1842, p. 3; Preface, *Songs by the Late John Hunt*, pp. 3–4.

127 'The Musical Festival', *Hereford Journal*, 30 August 1843, p. 3.

128 'Hereford Cathedral School', *Hereford Journal*, 14 December 1867, p. 8.

129 'Presentation', *Hereford Times*, 29 December 1860, p. 5.

130 'Hereford Festival. To the Editor of the *Hereford Journal*', *Hereford Journal*, 23 September 1846, p. 4.

131 'The Festival', *Hereford Times*, 18 September 1858, p. 8.

132 'The Hereford Choral Society', *Hereford Journal*, 16 June 1858, p. 5.

133 'Hereford Choral Society', *Hereford Times*, 22 April 1865, p. 7

134 'A letter dated 11 November 1850 from Mr G T Smith, Organist, on the subject of the Choral Service'. Chapter Acts, 14 November 1850; HCA 7031/20.

135 Chapter Acts, 14 November 1850; HCA 7031/20.

136 'George Townshend Smith', *The Musical Times*, Vol. 18, No 415 (September 1877), p. 427.

137 'Three Choirs Festival', *Glasgow Herald*, 4 September 1885, p. 7.

138 'The Hereford Festival', *Pall Mall Gazette*, 8 September 1885, p. 4.

139 'The Hereford Festival', *The Manchester Weekly Times*, 16 September 1882, p. 8

140 'Hereford Festival', *Worcester Journal*, 16 September 1882, p. 3.

141 'Death of Dr Langdon Colborne', *Gloucester Citizen*, 17 September 1889, p. 3.

142 'The Three Choirs Festival', *Gloucester Citizen*, 12 September 1888, p. 4.

143 'The Hereford Musical Festival', *The Musical Times*, Vol. 26, No 512 (October 1885), p. 595.

144 'Hereford Musical Festival', *The Musical Times*, Vol. 29, No 548 (October 1888), p. 604.

145 'Hereford Musical Festival', *Birmingham Daily Post*, 11 September 1888, p. 4.

146 'Death of Dr Langdon Colborne', *Gloucester Citizen*, 17 September 1889, p. 3.

147 Paul Iles, 'Music and Liturgy since 1600' in Gerald Aylmer and John Tiller (eds.), *Hereford Cathedral: a history* (London and Rio Grande, 2000), pp. 429–31.

148 Chapter Acts 4 October 1894; HCA, 7031/23, p. 223.

149 Chapter Acts 13 and 25 November 1907; HCA 7003/1/7, pp. 208–11.

150 'Dr G R Sinclair, Conductor of the Hereford Musical Festival', *The Musical Times*, Vol. 41, No 692 (October 1900), p. 662.

151 Trevor Beeson, *The Deans* (London, 2004), pp. 75–6.

152 'Dr G R Sinclair, Conductor of the Hereford Musical Festival', *The Musical Times*, Vol. 41, No 692 (October 1900), p. 662.

153 Unidentified cutting of a report of the annual meeting with the handwritten annotation 'Jan 29 1904'; HCA D865/1/2.

154 Beale, *Champagne and Shambles*, pp. 143–4.

155 Watkins Shaw, *The Three Choirs Festival: The Official History of the Meetings of the Three Choirs of Gloucester, Hereford and Worcester, c.1713–1953* (Worcester and London, 1954), p. 73.

156 Anon, *A Letter to a Country Gentleman on the subject of Methodism confined chiefly to its Causes, Progress and Consequences, in his own Neighbourhood* (Ipswich, 1805), pp. 32–3.

157 Percy A Scholes, under 'Methodism and Music', in *The Oxford Companion to Music* (Oxford/London/New York, 3/1941), p. 569.

158 John Hullah, *The Duty and Advantage of Learning to Sing*: A lecture delivered at the Leeds Church Institution on 19 February 1846 (London, 2/1846), p. 20.

159 Percy A Scholes, *The Mirror of Music 1844–1944*, Vol. 1 (London, 1947), p. 13.

160 http://www.herefordshire.gov.uk/factsandfigures/docs/research/ current_hfds_population_digest.pdf; accessed 13 January 2012.

161 Elgar, *A Future for English Music*, p. 125.

162 'Mr G R Sinclair and his Doctor's Robes', *Royal Cornwall Gazette*, 30 November 1899, p. 5.

163 'Hereford Choral Society', *Gloucester Citizen*, 28 November 1901, p. 4.

164 'Hereford Choral Society', *Worcestershire Chronicle*, 29 November 1902, p. 5.

CHAPTER II

1 This information in a letter from J B Pilley read out at the annual meeting on 30 January 1903. Minute Book 1891–1923; HCA D865/1/2.

2 Names listed on the back of an 1863 programme leaflet. Programme leaflets 1852–1904; HCA 865/3/4.

3 Reports of the annual meetings, Minute Book 1891–1923; HCA D865/1/2.

4 Typed report of the annual meeting on 1 February 1924. Minute Book 1924–69; HCA D865/1/3.

5 Chorus names listed in the programme books for the *Gerontius* performances (7 October 1989 and 20 November 2004) and for the performance of the Monteverdi *Vespers* (13 March 1999); HCA D865/865/4/2.

6 Chorus names listed in the programme book for the Verdi *Requiem* performance on 17 March 2012.

7 http://www.bbc.co.uk/herefordandworcester/musicmap/venues/hillside_ ballroom_hereford/content/index.html; accessed 14 January 2013.

8 'Sullivan's *The Golden Legend*', *Cheltenham Looker-On*, 7 March 1896, p. 11.

9 Anthony Boden, *Three Choirs: a History of the Festival* (Stroud, 1992), p. 269.

10 Unidentified cutting of a report of the 1904 annual meeting with the handwritten annotation 'Jan 29 1904'. Minute Book 1891–1923; HCA D865/1/2.

11 Unidentified cutting of a report of the annual meeting with the handwritten annotation '2 Feb 1906'. Minute Book 1891–1923; HCA D865/1/2.

12 *The Organ*, No 328, May–July 2004, p. 50.

13 Lists of concert attendances from November 1999 to March 2012 filed in the Minute Book 2005– .

14 'Exeter Oratorio Society's Festival', *Western Times*, 3 April 1913, p. 2.

15 'Philharmonic Concert', *Hereford Journal*, 24 December 1853.

16 E Wulstan Atkins, *The Elgar-Atkins Friendship* (London, 1984), p. 27.

17 William Collins, *A Short History of Hereford* (Hereford, 1913), p. 9.

18 'Music in Hereford', *The Musical Times*, Vol. 40, No 675 (May 1899), pp. 330–31.

19 Unidentified cutting reporting the 1929 annual meeting. Minute Book 1924–69; HCA D865/1/3.

20 Letter from the Music Director writing for Programme Director, Midland Region, BBC Birmingham to Percy Hull dated 9 May 1935. Percy Hull papers (correspondence 1934–35); HCA D865/5/3.

21 Hereford Choral Society papers: Orchestra da camera file.

22 'Hereford Choral Society', *Hereford Times*, 15 January 1842, p. 3.

23 'Royal Academy of Music … Female Department', *London Daily News* 27 July 1874, p. 5.

24 H Saxe Wyndham and Geoffrey L'Epine (eds), *Who's Who in Music: a biographical record of contemporary musicians* (London, 2/1915), p. 268.

25 *Littlebury's Directory and Gazetteer of Herefordshire*, 1876–7.

26 Leaflet for concert on 2 May 1878; HCA D865/4/1.

27 Joseph Foster, *Alumni Oxonienses* (1715–1886) (Oxford, 1888); *Herefordshire Portraits* (Hereford, 1908), p. 49.

28 'Concert in Aid of the Funds for the Restoration of the Parish Church', *Hereford Times*, 4 July 1863, p. 6.

29 *Hereford Times*, 6 October 1866.

30 Hereford Cathedral Archives 30.B.32; 'Worcester Festival Choral Society's Concert', *Worcester Journal*, 25 January 1896, p. 3.

31 'Tamworth Choral Society. The Messiah', *Tamworth Herald*, 19 March 1892, p. 5.

32 'Gloucester Choral Society. Last Concert of the Season', *Gloucester Citizen*, 23 March 1881, p. 3.

33 Aneurin Thomas, *Con Molto Piacere: 150 years of singing with the Hereford Choral Society* (Hereford, 1987), p. 63; Wyndham and L'Epine (eds), *Who's Who in Music*, p. 219.

34   'From Wesley to Elgar', *The Times*, 27 November 1937.

35   Boden, *Three Choirs: a History of the Festival*, p. 191.

36   Boden, *Three Choirs: a History of the Festival*, pp. 83–3, 91.

37   http://www.simonwall.co.uk/biog.html; accessed 11 January 2013.

38   Minutes of the meeting of 14 October 1940. Minute Book 1924–69; HCA D865/1/3; Letters from Dean Waterfield to Percy Hull dated 10 October 1940; from the Secretary but signed by P Hull to Dean Waterfield dated 17 October 1940; from Dean Waterfield to the Choral Society Secretary dated 21 October 1940. Percy Hull correspondence 1938–41; HCA D865/5/6.

39   Unidentified cutting of a report of the Annual Meeting annotated 'Feb 1/95'. Minute Book 1891–1923; HCA D865/1/2. Also in the printed report of the Choral Society for the 1904 season. Printed annual reports and accounts 1902–1910; HCA D865/2/2.

40   'Music in Hereford', *The Musical Times*, Vol. 40, No 675 (May 1899), pp. 330–31.

41   Unidentified cutting of a report of the annual meeting with the handwritten annotation 'Jan 29 1904'. Minute Book 1891–1923. HCA D865/1/2.

42   Typed minutes of the AGM on 1 February 1924. Minute Book 1924–69; HCA D865/1/3.

43   Unidentified cutting of 23 January 1929 reporting the recent AGM. Minute Book 1924–69; HCA D865/1/3.

44   'Choral Society. Hereford Choir's Brilliant Work'. Unidentified cutting giving an account of the 1928 annual meeting. Minute Book 1924–69; HCA D865/1/3.

45   *Hereford Times*, 7 February 1931. Cutting in Minute Book 1924–69; HCA D865/1/3.

46   David Manning (ed), *Vaughan Williams On Music* (New York, 2008), p. 113.

47   Letter from Arthur Cranmer to P C Hull dated 26 November 1937. Percy Hull papers, letters after the performance of *The Dream of Gerontius* in 1937; HCA D865/5/5.

48   H C Colles, *Walford Davies* (Oxford, 1942), pp. 73–4.

49   Information supplied by Roy Massey; see also: Lindsay Lafford, 'Festival memories from the 1920s', *Three Choirs Festival Programme Book*, Hereford 2012, pp. 219–22.

50   L R B, 'Bristol Choral Society. A Successful Broadcast Performance', *Western Daily Press*, 14 April 1934, p. 9.

51   Thomas, *Con Molto Piacere*, p. 63.

52   From an un-dated typed *Constitution* filed with minutes of committee meetings in 1993.

53   Minutes of the committee meeting held on 6 September 1989.

54   Minutes of the Annual General Meeting on 28 October 1996, AGM Minute file 1988–2003.

55   Committee meeting of 9 October 2006; Minute Book 2005/6–2011/12.

56   Unidentified un-dated cutting from 1944. Miscellaneous press cutting; HCA D865/10

57   'Edward Elgar' in Percy M Young (ed), *A Future for English Music* (London, 1968), p. 135.

58   Printed booklet: Rules of the Hereford Choral Society (as revised on 2 February 1900). Stuck into the Minute Book 1891–1923; HCA D865/1/2.

59   J A Rodgers, 'An Analysis of Choral Tone', *The Musical Times*, Vol. 53, No 833 (July 1912), pp. 440–42.

60   Letter to Percy Hull dated 26 November 1937 from W A Symonds, Bedford. Percy Hull Papers. Correspondence following the performance of *The Dream of Gerontius*; HCA D865/5/5.

61   'From Wesley to Elgar', *The Times*, 27 November 1937.

62   Michael Kennedy, *Portrait of Elgar* (London, 2/1982), pp. 178–9.

63   'C.', 'An Elgar Concert', *The Musical Times*, Vol. 67, No 1000 (June 1926), p. 550.

64   Herbert Sumsion, 'Percy Clarke Hull 1878–1968: a tribute', Hereford Festival Programme Book 1970, p. 22.

65   See Jerrold Northrop Moore's comments in the liner notes of the three-CD set: The Elgar Society, *Elgar's Interpreters on Record*, Vol. 5, Elgar Editions EECD003–5 [issued 2007].

66   H C Colles in *The Times*, 4 March 1929; reproduced in Jerrold Northrop Moore, *Edward Elgar: A Creative Life* (London, 1987), p. 779.

67   R A Edwards, *And the Glory: The Huddersfield Choral Society 1836–1986* (Leeds, 1985), p. 145.

68   L P Wilkinson, *A Century of King's 1873–1972* (Cambridge, 1980), p. 95.

69   Timothy Day, 'English cathedral music in the twentieth century' in *The Cambridge Companion to Singing* ed. John Potter (Cambridge University Press, 2000), pp. 123–32; Timothy Day, 'Tudor Church Music in the Twentieth Century' in *A Discography of Tudor Church Music* (The British Library, 1989), pp. 15–48; Timothy Day, 'The establishment of choral scholarships at King's College, Cambridge', *Journal of the Royal College of Organists*, Vol. 2 (New Series), 2008, pp. 64–73.

70   It was Percy Bulmer who was to found H P Bulmer, the cider-making company in Hereford, in 1887.

71   A note from Henry Leslie to the Philharmonic Society Committee dated 22 December 1886; HRO A63/IV/30/9.

72   Thomas, *Con Molto Piacere*, p. 33.

73   George C Martin, *The Art of Training Choir Boys* (London, 1892[?]), p. 21.

74   See, for example, *The Musical Times*, Vol. 308, No 557 (July 1889), p. 385.

75   Reprinted from *The Times*, 16 August 1945 in *English Church Music*, Vol. xv, No 4, October 1945, p. 27.

76   http://www.herefordcathedral.org/music/choir/choral-scholarships; accessed 13 January 2013.

77   Edward Elgar, *A Future for English Music and other lectures* edited by Percy M Young (London, 1968), p. 125.

78   E Greenfield, R Layton, and I March, *The Penguin Guide to Compact Discs and Cassettes* (London, 1992), p. 359.

79   *The Monthly Letter*, July 1957, p. 7.

80   Quoted in Jerrold Northrop Moore, *Elgar on Record* (London, 1974), p. 84.

81   'St Martin's New Church', *Hereford Times*, 16 October 1841, p. 3.

82   Quoted by Denis Stevens in 'A Soupcon of Vibrato', *High Fidelity Magazine*, Vol. 14, No 1, January 1964, p. 110.

83   Minutes for the AGM on 29 October 1990; AGM Minute file 1988–2003.

84   Watkins Shaw, *The Succession of Organists* (Oxford, 1991), p. 143.

85   Thomas, *Con Molto Piacere*, pp. 33–42; Alexander Brent-Smith, 'Sir Percy Hull's Retirement', *Musical Times*, Vol. 90, No 1280 (October 1949), p. 361; Herbert Sumsion, 'Percy Clarke Hull 1878–1968: a tribute', Hereford Festival Programme Book 1970, p. 22.

86   Boden, *Three Choirs: a History of the Festival*, pp. 193–4.

87 Meredith Davies's recollections quoted in Boden, *Three Choirs: a History of the Festival*, p. 193.

88 William Owen ed, *A Life in Music: conversations with Sir David Willcocks and Friends* (Oxford/New York, 2008), p. 105.

89 http://www.telegraph.co.uk/news/obituaries/1486929/Meredith-Davies.html; accessed 12 September 2012; http://www.independent.co.uk/news/obituaries/meredith-davies-6151239.html; accessed 12 September 2012.

90 H P Allen, Notes for a speech or article: New College, Oxford archives: 'Choral music in wartime'; New College Archives PA/ALL, 5/2.

91 Isaac Williams, *On reserve in communicating religious knowledge* (Tracts for the times, No 80), (London, 1838), p. 55.

92 http://herefordshire.greatbritishlife.co.uk/article/herefordshire-people-geraint-bowen-musicman-7021/; accessed 12 September 2012.

93 Basil Ramsey, 'Close to Music: Melville Cook looks back in conversation with Basil Ramsey', *The Musical Times*, Vol. 133, No 1798 (December 1992), pp. 663–5; Address given by Donald Hunt at the memorial service to Melville Cook in Gloucester Cathedral on 17 July 1993, a leaflet kindly copied by Michael Trott.

94 Private communication from Duncan Wilkins.

95 Paul Iles, 'Music and Liturgy since 1600' in Gerald Aylmer and John Tiller (eds.), *Hereford Cathedral: a history* (London and Rio Grande, 2000), p. 438.

96 Philip Barrett, 'From Victorian to Modern Times, 1832–1982), in ibid., p. 182.

97 Thomas, *Con Molto Piacere*, pp. 52, 54.

98 Ibid., pp. 55–7.

99 Minutes of the Committee meeting of 6 September 1989.

100 From lists of the conductor's rehearsal comments compiled by 'Seligra'; Jo Swindells' private papers.

101 Thomas, *Con Molto Piacere*, p. 58–66.

102 A draft for the wording for a card to be presented to Dr Massey on his retirement. Private papers of Jo Swindells.

103 William McVicker, liner-notes to *The English Anthem*, Vol. 8, Hyperion CDA67483 [released 2005], p. 3.

104 Obituary in *The Times*, 6 March 1998; obituary in *The Independent*, by Andrew Green, 25 February 1998 (http://www.independent.co.uk/news/obituaries/obituary-martindale-sidwell-1146846.html; accessed 15 October 2012.

105 Comment on the introduction of 'scrambling' in the Conductor's Report in the Minutes of the AGM on 18 October 2010. Minute file 2005/6– .

106 Sheet headed '1935, Finance'. Minute Book, 1924–69; HCA D865/1/3.

107 Lindsay Lafford (assistant accompanist *c* 1929–34); http://lord-of-ridley.com/bio.htm; accessed 2 March 2013; 'Mr Lindsay A Lafford ARCO', *Hereford Times*, 27 January 1934, p. 8.

108 David Briggs (1985–88); advertisement for the Gloucester Choral Society, Hereford Three Choirs Festival programme book 2000, p. 60.

109 Robert Green (1968–84), http://www.leominsterchoralsociety.co.uk/page44.html; accessed 12 February 2013.

110 Huw Williams (1995–8); http://www.cantemus.co.uk/huw-williams.html; accessed 1 March 2013.

111 Percy Hull (? –1914) and Geraint Bowen (1989–94).

112 Unidentified cutting annotated 'Oct. 7th 1921', a report of the 1921 annual meeting. Minute Book 1891–1923; HCA D865/1/2.

113 AGM on 28 October 1996.

114 Descriptions of the committee given by Roy Massey at AGMs on 17 October 1988 and 29 October 1990.

115 Percy Hull papers, mainly correspondence 1934–49; HCA D865/5

116 Un-dated letter [but of November 1936] from P C Hull to Stainer & Bell regarding hire of material for Stanford's *Songs of the Fleet*; HCA D865/17.

117 Letter from the Secretary but signed by P Hull to Dean Waterfield dated 17 October 1940. Percy Hull correspondence 1938–41; HCA D865/5/6.

118 Thomas, *Con Molto Piacere*, p. 56.

119 List of the Society's officers given in the programme for the concert on 17 November 2012.

120 Thomas, *Con Molto Piacere* pp. 38–9.

121 Ibid., p. 63.

122 Ibid., p. 22.

123 Letter from Edward Elgar to Nicholas Heins dated 5 October 1882 quoted in: 'When Elgar played for £2.12.6.' 'This week's Midland broadcast of the Hereford Choral Society's performance of *The Dream of Gerontius* gives topicality to these glimpses of Elgar's life': *Radio Times* dated 19 November 1937, p. 15.

124 Thomas, *Con Molto Piacere*, p. 19.

125 *Hereford Times*, 8 February 1933.

126 Hereford Choral Society: Charity Number 508140; registered 13 February 1979.

127 A letter to the *Hereford Times*, 2 February 1918 from VERITAS states that Sinclair conducted without any fee.

128 Minutes of the Choral Society's Committee Meeting of 27 May 1994; Thomas, *Con Molto Piacere*, p. 54.

129 Unattributed cutting reporting the 1927 Annual General Meeting: Minute Book 1924–69; HCA D865/1/3.

130 Rule V of the *Rules of the Hereford Choral Society*, [as revised 2 February 1900], printed booklet, stuck into Minute Book 1891–1923; HCA D865/1/2.

131 Ibid., pp. 60–63.

132 Chairman's report of COMSOC, 28 October 1996 with the minutes of the Annual General Meeting on 28 October 1996; AGM Minute File for 1988–2003.

133 Auction lists for 8 March 2001 and 1 March 2006 both in the auction administration file for 2006.

134 Committee meeting of 7 February 2005.

135 *Income and expenditure account* for year ending 31 August 2001, AGM Minute File for 1988–2003.

136 Income and expenditure account for year ending 31 August 2006, Minute File for 2005/6–2011/12.

137 Committee meeting of 18 February 2002.

138 Committee meeting of 30 January 1995.

139 Committee Meeting of 16 April 1997.

140 Thomas, *Con Molto Piacere*, p. 59.

141 Committee Meeting of 12 March 2001.

142 'Dotted Crotchet', 'Hereford Cathedral', *The Musical Times*, Vol. 47, No 757 (March 1906), p. 169.

143 'Sir Edward Elgar. Death of the Great British Composer', *Hereford Times*, 24 February 1934, p. 9.

144 Melville Cook's recollections quoted in Boden, *Three Choirs: a History of the Festival*, p. 179.

145 Vera Hockman, quoted in Jerrold Northrop Moore, *Edward Elgar: a Creative Life* (Oxford, 1984), p. 793.

146 'From Wesley to Elgar', *The Times*, 27 November 1937.

147 Ernest Newman, *The Nation*, 16 November 1910, quoted in Diana McVeagh, Preface to the Eulenberg miniature score of the Violin Concerto (London, 1989), p. vi.

148 'Cathedral Music', *Hereford Journal*, 31 August 1836, p. 4.

149 'Miscellanea', *Hereford Journal*, 23 March 1836, p. 4.

150 A letter dated 22 February 1927 from Elgar to Randall Davidson, in *Letters of a Lifetime* (Oxford, 1990), p. 397.

151 Christopher Palmer, *Herbert Howells: a study* (Borough Green, Sevenoaks, 1978), p. 17.

152 Film directed by John Bridcut, *The Passions of Vaughan Williams* (BBC Four, 2008).

153 Peter Levi, *The flutes of autumn* (London, 1983), p. 80.

154 Ralph Vaughan Williams in '[National music:] some conclusions', in *National music and other essays* (Oxford, 2/1986), p. 63.

155 Ralph Vaughan Williams, 'The evolution of the folk-song', *National music and other essays* (Oxford, 2/1986), p. 39.

156 Ralph Vaughan Williams, *National music and other essays* (Oxford, 2/1986), p. 67.

157 Ralph Vaughan Williams, 'A Minim's Rest', *National Music and other essays* (London, 2/1987), p. 154.

158 Ralph Vaughan Williams, 'What is Music', *National Music and other essays* (London, 2/1987), p. 206.

159 Ralph Vaughan Williams, 'Gustav Holst: an Essay and a Note', *National Music and other essays* (London, 2/1987), p. 151.

160 Frans Brüggen, in an interview conducted on 22 March 1977 at Ann Arbor, Michigan, in John Harvith and Susan Edwards Harvith (eds), *Edison, Musicians, and the Phonograph: A Century in Retrospect* (New York, Westport, Connecticut, London, 1987), p. 204.

161 Ralph Vaughan Williams, 'How Do We Make Music?' *National Music and other essays* (London, 2/1987), p. 223.

162 Donald Tovey and Geoffrey Parratt, *Walter Parratt: Master of Music* (London, 1941), p. 67.

163 Ralph Vaughan Williams, 'A Musical Autobiography', *National Music and other essays* (London, 2/1987), p. 183.

164 Edward Dannreuther, *Musical Ornamentation* (London, 1893), Vol. I, p. vii.

165 Ralph Vaughan Williams, 'Bach, the Great Bourgeois', *National Music and other essays* (London, 2/1987), p. 176.

166 G M Trevelyan, *A Layman's Love of Letters* (London, 1954), pp. 124–5.

167 G M Trevelyan, *Garibaldi and the Making of Italy* (London, 1911) p. 297.

168 'Glocester [*sic*] Musical Festival', *Hereford Journal* 19 September 1838, p. 3.

169 'As it is even now time that some definite arrangements with reference to the ensuing meeting of the three choirs of Gloucester, Hereford, and Worcester Cathedrals …' *Hereford Journal* 28 April 1841, p. 3.

170 'Progress at Chepstow', *Hereford Journal*, 28 November 1849, p. 3.

171 Printed account of AGM of 1 October 1920: Minute Book 1891–1923; HCA D865/1/2.

172 Waldo Selden Pratt, 'The Isolation of Music', *Proceedings of the Musical Association* Twenty-First Session 1894–95, p. 166.

173 Unidentified cutting of a report of the Annual Meeting with the written annotation '1st October 1920'. Minute Book 1891–1923; HCA D865/1/2.

174 Cutting from the *Hereford Times*, 18 February 1927. Minute Book 1924–69; HCA D865/1/3.

175 Cutting with handwritten annotation 'Hereford Times 7 Feb 1931', 'Annual Meeting of the Hereford Choral Society'. Minute Book 1924–69; HCA D865/1/3.

176 Letter dated 29 November 1937 from Carice Elgar Blake to Percy Hull; HCA D865/5/5. Correspondence following the performance of *The Dream of Gerontius*.

177 Typed report of the AGM 1 February 1924. Minute Book 1924–69; HCA D865/1/3.

178 E Wulstan Atkins, *The Elgar-Atkins Friendship* (London, 1984), p. 341.

179 Letter to Percy Hull from Margaret Beith dated 26 November 1937. Percy Hull papers: correspondence following the performance of *The Dream of Gerontius*; HCA D865/5/5.

180 Sermon for the 150th anniversary of the Hereford Choral Society preached in Hereford Cathedral by Paul Iles on 8 November 1987; HCA D865/6.

181 *Hereford Times*, 15 March 2001.

182 Mihaly Csikszentmihalyi, *Flow* (London 1992, revised/2002), pp. 3–4.

183 Typed letter from Christabel Hopton to Sir Percy Hull dated 17 January 1948. Percy Hull Papers, correspondence 1948; HCA D865/5/9; *Who's Who in Herefordshire* (Hereford: Wilson & Phillips, 1933), p. 64.

List of illustrations

The illustrations are from the Hereford Cathedral archives [HCA] (these copied by Gordon Taylor), from the Foxton Archive [DFA], from the Hereford County Record Office, or taken specially by Dr Derek Foxton or Gordon Taylor. I am most grateful to the photographers, to the County Record Office, to the Dean and Chapter and to Dr Foxton for permission to reproduce material. The title-page of Elgar's *Te Deum* and *Benedictus* is reproduced by kind permission of Lady Hull's executors, Lambe Corner, Solicitors, Hereford.

Index